William Blackwood and Sons

Family Prayers

William Blackwood and Sons
Family Prayers
ISBN/EAN: 9783337275129

Printed in Europe, USA, Canada, Australia, Japan

Cover: Foto ©Lupo / pixelio.de

More available books at **www.hansebooks.com**

Aids to Devotion

FAMILY PRAYERS

PREPARED BY

A SPECIAL COMMITTEE

AND AUTHORISED BY THE

General Assembly of the Church of Scotland

TO WHICH IS PREFIXED

By Authority

A PASTORAL LETTER FROM THE GENERAL ASSEMBLY
ON FAMILY WORSHIP

A NEW EDITION

WILLIAM BLACKWOOD AND SONS
EDINBURGH AND LONDON
MDCCCLXXXII

Preface.

THE Committee of the General Assembly on Aids to Devotion was originally appointed in 1849, for the purpose of drawing up forms of Social Worship, according to the usage of the National Church of Scotland, for *Soldiers, Sailors, Colonists, and other persons who are deprived of the ordinary services of a Christian Ministry.* In pursuance of this object, the Committee published in 1859, a collection of 'Prayers for Social and Family Worship,' which, having speedily attained a very wide diffusion, and met with a highly gratifying appreciation among the members of the Church, both at home and in the colonies, received in 1863 the sanction of the General Assembly.

Encouraged by the favourable reception of their previous labours, and urged by numerous solicitatations which were addressed to them, the Committee were induced to prepare another volume, consisting exclusively of Prayers for Family Worship, and adapted, not to any particular class, but to the general circumstances of all Christian households. In doing so, they availed themselves of the

Family Prayers contained in their previous publication. But these were supplemented by a great number of additional prayers, which the General Assembly of 1864 allowed to be appended to them, so as to render the work more generally acceptable and useful as a MANUAL OF FAMILY DEVOTION. And there was prefixed to the collection, by authority, a *Pastoral Letter of the General Assembly to the People of Scotland on Family Worship.*

In complying with the demand for a New Edition of this volume, the Committee cannot refrain from expressing their gratification with the large measure of public support and approbation which it has already received. They have also peculiar satisfaction in announcing, that it is now re-issued, not as hitherto with the mere permission, but (as will be seen from the annexed Deliverance) *with the authority and hearty recommendation* of the Supreme Ecclesiastical Court of the Church of Scotland. And their earnest prayer is, that it may, by the blessing of God, be greatly conducive to the furtherance of domestic piety throughout the land.

In name of the Committee,

THOS. J. CRAWFORD, D.D.
Convener.

N.B.—*Some passages in the prayers are enclosed within brackets, to indicate that they may be omitted, either when they are unsuitable, or when greater brevity is desired.*

Deliverances of the General Assembly of the Church of Scotland on the Reports of their Committee on Aids to Devotion.

At Edinburgh, the Third day of June Eighteen hundred and sixty-seven,

The which day, the General Assembly of the Church of Scotland being met and constituted, *inter alia,* the Assembly called for the Report of the Committee on Aids to Devotion, which was given in and read by Dr Crawford, the Convener.

It was moved, and seconded, and unanimously agreed to, that—

The General Assembly approve of the Report, and reappoint the Committee, with Dr Crawford as their Convener; and instruct them, along with the Committee on Army and Navy Chaplains, to prepare and publish a small and portable selection from the 'Prayers for Social and Family Worship,' for the use of Presbyterians in the Army and Navy.

The General Assembly learn with satisfaction, that the Collection of Family Prayers for Four Weeks, and for Sacramental and other special occasions, has been attended with a remarkable measure of success. They authorise the Committee to stereotype this volume, so that it may be published at a lower price; and they heartily recommend the use of it to those who may require such aid to Family Devotion.

Extracted from the Records of the General Assembly of the Church of Scotland by

  (Signed) JOHN COOK, *Cl. Eccl. Scot.*

DELIVERANCES.

At Edinburgh, the Twenty-ninth day of May Eighteen hundred and sixty-four,

The which day, the General Assembly of the Church of Scotland being met and constituted, *inter alia*, the General Assembly, on an application from Dr Crawford, the Convener of the Committee on Aids to Devotion, authorised the said Committee to prefix to the Family Prayers about to be issued the 'Pastoral Address of the General Assembly to the People of Scotland on Family Worship.'

Extracted from the Records of the General Assembly of the Church of Scotland by

(Signed) JOHN COOK, *Cl. Eccl. Scot.*

At Edinburgh, the Thirty-first day of May Eighteen hundred and sixty-nine,

The General Assembly instruct the Committee on Aids to Devotion to reprint, in a cheap form, the Pastoral Address of 1836 on Domestic Devotion; and the General Assembly enjoin all the Ministers of this Church to take care that said Pastoral Address be read from the pulpit on the first Sabbath after they have received it; and that on that occasion the General Assembly's 'Family Prayers' be recommended to the use of the Members of the Church.

Extracted from the Records of the General Assembly of the Church of Scotland by

(Signed) JOHN COOK, *Cl. Eccl. Scot.*

Members

of the

Committee of the General Assembly on Aids to Devotion.

THE MODERATOR.
Rev. JOHN PAUL, D.D., St Cuthbert's, Edinburgh.
... JAMES VEITCH, D.D., St Cuthbert's, Edinburgh.
... JAMES GRANT, D.D. D.C.L., Oxon., St Mary's Church, Edinburgh.
... WILLIAM GLOVER, D.D., Greenside Church, Edinburgh.
... WILLIAM STEVENSON, D.D., Professor of Ecclesiastical History, Edinburgh.
... DAVID ARNOT, D.D., High Church, Edinburgh.
... THOMAS J. CRAWFORD, D.D., Professor of Divinity, Edinburgh.
... A. H. CHARTERIS, D.D., Professor of Biblical Criticism, Edinburgh.
... ROBERT NISBET, D.D., West St Giles's Church, Edinburgh.
... WILLIAM ROBERTSON, D.D., New Greyfriars' Church, Edinburgh.
... MAXWELL NICHOLSON, D.D., St Stephen's Church, Edinburgh.
... WILLIAM H. GRAY, D.D., Lady Yester's Church, Edinburgh.
... ROBERT WALLACE, D.D., Old Greyfriars' Church, Edinburgh.
... JOHN STUART, St Andrew's Church, Edinburgh.
... JAMES E. CUMMING, Newington Church, Edinburgh.
... WILLIAM SMITH, D.D., North Leith.
... JAMES MITCHELL, M.A., South Leith.

COMMITTEE ON AIDS TO DEVOTION.

Rev. J. M'Murtrie, M.A., St Bernard's, Edinburgh.
... W. L. Colvin, D.D., Cramond.
... John Cook, D.D., Haddington.
... W. Lee, D.D., Roxburgh.
... W. L. Riach, M.A., Pencaitland.
... Robert Wright, D.D., Dalkeith.
... Thomas Gordon, D.D., Newbattle.
... Norman Macleod, D.D., Barony Church, Glasgow.
... James Craik, D.D., St George's Church, Glasgow.
... Robert Jamieson, D.D., St Paul's Church, Glasgow.
... D. Runciman, D.D., St Andrew's Church, Glasgow.
... J. R. Macduff, D.D., Sandyford Church, Glasgow.
... Donald Macleod, B.A., Park Church, Glasgow.
... Principal Barclay, D.D., University of Glasgow.
... M. Leishman, D.D., Govan.
... Principal Tulloch, D.D., St Mary's College, St Andrews.
... F. Crombie, D.D., Professor of Biblical Criticism, St Andrews.
... A. Mitchell, D.D., Professor of Ecclesiastical History, St Andrews.
... A. K. H. Boyd, D.D., St Andrews.
... Principal Campbell, D.D., University of Aberdeen.
... W. R. Pirie, D.D., Professor of Ecclesiastical History, Aberdeen.
... S. Trail, LL.D. D.D., Professor of Divinity, Aberdeen.
... W. Milligan, D.D., Professor of Biblical Criticism, Aberdeen.
... James Forsyth, D.D., West Church, Aberdeen.
... John Macleod, D.D., Morven.
... James M'Culloch, D.D., Greenock.
... F. L. Robertson, Greenock.
... Thomas M'Kie, Erskine.
... James Maitland, D.D., Kells.
... Thomas Liddell, D.D., Lochmaben.
... James Charles, D.D., Kirkowen.
... P. H. Keith, D.D., Hamilton.
... Paton J. Gloag, D.D., Blantyre.
... John Macrae, D.D., Hawick.
... R. Stevenson, Dalry.
... K. M. Phin, D.D., Galashiels.
... James Cochrane, Cupar-Fife.
... Archibald Watson, D.D., Dundee.
... W. Ritchie, D.D., Longforgan.

COMMITTEE ON AIDS TO DEVOTION.

Rev. JAMES S. BARTY. D.D., Bendochy.
... J. G. YOUNG, Monifieth.
... D. M'DONALD, D.D., Inverness.
... JAMES SELLAR, D.D., Aberlour.
... FRANCIS WYLIE, D.D., Elgin.
... J. M'DONALD, D.D., Comrie.
... JOHN CLARK, D.D., Dunoon.
... GEORGE COOK, D.D., Kincardine O'Neil.
... R. H. STORY, Roseneath.
... DUNCAN CAMPBELL, North Knapdale.
... S. CAMERON, M.A., Logierait.
... GEORGE ALEXANDER, Stirling.
... ARCHIBALD CLERK, Kilmalie.
... GEORGE COOK, M.A., Borgue.
... JAMES MACGREGOR, D.D., Tron Church, Edinburgh.
The Right Honourable the EARL OF SELKIRK.
The Right Honourable the EARL OF SEAFIELD.
The Right Honourable the EARL OF STAIR.
The Honourable LORD POLWARTH.
The Honourable LORD JERVISWOODE.
Sir W. JARDINE, Bart.
Sir J. H. MAXWELL, Bart.
Sir ROBERT ANSTRUTHER, Bart.
Sir W. BAILLIE, Bart.
Sir GEORGE GRANT SUTTIE, Bart.
Major the Honourable ROBERT BAILLIE.
JAMES JOHNSTONE, Esq. of Alva.
R. LEE, Esq., Procurator for the Church.
JOHN TAIT, Esq., Sheriff of Clackmannan.
GEORGE DEMPSTER, Esq. of Skibo.
JAMES HOPE, Esq., Deputy-Keeper of the Signet.
ARCHIBALD C. SWINTON, Esq. of Kimmerghame.
JOHN SMITH, Esq., M.D., Edinburgh.
DAVID SMITH, Esq., W.S., Edinburgh.
HUGH BARCLAY, Esq., Sheriff-Substitute of Perthshire.
ISAAC BAYLEY, Esq., Edinburgh.

THOMAS J. CRAWFORD, D.D.,
Convener.

Contents.

	PAGE
THE GENERAL ASSEMBLY'S PASTORAL LETTER TO THE PEOPLE OF SCOTLAND ON FAMILY WORSHIP, . .	1

PRAYERS FOR FAMILY WORSHIP—

Introductory Prayers, ... 10
Concluding Prayers, ... 19

First Week.

Lord's Day Morning...Prayer for grace to hallow the Sabbath, ... 20
———*Evening*...Thanksgiving for privileges, and prayer for grace to walk worthy of them, . . . 23
Monday Morning ......Prayer for grace to carry the influence of the Sabbath into the business of the week, . . 26
———*Evening*........Prayer to God as our Father, . . 28
Tuesday Morning.......Prayer for Divine guidance and guardianship throughout the day,* 30
———*Evening*.........Prayer for the Divine blessing and protection during the night,† 32

---

* Calvin's 'Morning Prayer,' slightly altered.
† Calvin's 'Evening Prayer,' with some additions.

First Week—Continued.

Wednesday Morning...General thanksgiving,	34
———*Evening*.....Prayer for a due sense of the Divine goodness,	37
Thursday Morning.....Prayer for a sense of God's presence,	39
———*Evening*......Prayer for pardon and repentance,	42
Friday Morning........Prayer for God's help and blessing in our ordinary occupations,	45
———*Evening*.........Prayer for heavenly-mindedness,	48
Saturday Morning......Prayer for sanctification,	50
———*Evening*......Review of life and preparation for death,	52

Second Week.

Lord's Day Morning...General confession and supplication,	55
———*Evening*...Confession of imperfections, and prayer for growth in grace,	58
Monday Morning.......Prayer for grace to walk with God in our several callings,	60
———*Evening*........Prayer for trust in God,	62
Tuesday Morning.......Prayer for temporal mercies,	64
———*Evening*.......Prayer for contentment,	66
Wednesday Morning....Prayer for faith in Christ,	68
———*Evening*.....Prayer for love to God,	70
Thursday Morning.....Prayer for the mortification of sin,	72
———*Evening*.....Prayer for the Holy Spirit,	74
Friday Morning.........Prayer for Divine help and guidance throughout the day,*	76
———*Evening*..........Prayer for the Divine forgiveness and guardianship,†	78
Saturday Morning......Thanksgiving for the goodness of God, and prayer for love to men,	80
———*Evening*.......Prayer for perseverance,	82

---

* From Jeremy Taylor. † Ibid.

Third Week.

Lord's Day Morning...Praise for ordinances, and prayer for grace to profit by them,	85
———*Evening*....Prayer for a profitable use of God's Word,	88
Monday Morning.......Prayer for grace to serve God in our daily life,	91
———*Evening*.......Prayer for pardon and repentance,	93
Tuesday Morning.......Prayer for faith,	96
———*Evening*.......Prayer for hope,	98
Wednesday Morning...Prayer for charity,	100
———*Evening*....Prayer for inward peace,	102
Thursday Morning.....Prayer for conformity to Christ,	104
———*Evening*.....Prayer for self-denial,	106
Friday Morning.........Prayer for temporal mercies,	108
———*Evening*.........Thanksgiving,	110
Saturday Morning......Prayer for grace to fill our station aright,	112
———*Evening*.........Prayer for grace to seek the things that are above,	114

Fourth Week.

Lord's Day Morning...Praise, confession, and supplication,	116
———*Evening* ...Praise for the light and grace of the Gospel,	119
Monday Morning.......Prayer for habitual fellowship with God,	122
———*Evening*.......Prayer for self-knowledge and watchfulness,	124
Tuesday Morning.......Prayer for self-government in heart, speech, and action,	126
———*Evening*........Prayer for trust in Divine providence,	129
Wednesday Morning...Prayer for meekness and peaceableness,	131
———*Evening*....Prayer for love to Christ,	133

Fourth Week—*Continued*

Thursday Morning......Prayer for grace to live a godly, righteous, and sober life, ... 135
———*Evening*......Prayer for patience and contentment, ... 138
Friday Morning.........Prayer for earnestness in religious duties, ... 140
———*Evening*.........Prayer for humility, . . . 142
Saturday Morning......Prayer to be enlightened and established in the knowledge of the truth, . . . 144
———*Evening*......Prayer for grace to consider our latter end, ... 147

PRAYERS FOR SACRAMENTAL AND OTHER SPECIAL OCCASIONS.

Morning of a Sacramental Fast Day, ... 150
Evening of a Sacramental Fast Day, ... 153
Morning of a Communion Sabbath, ... 156
Evening of a Communion Sabbath, ... 159
First Morning of the Year, ... 162
Last Evening of the Year, ... 166
Morning Prayer for a Family visited with Sickness or any other Affliction, ... 169
Evening Prayer for a Family visited with Sickness or any other Affliction, ... 172
Morning Prayer for a Bereaved Family, ... 175
Evening Prayer for a Bereaved Family, ... 177

The General Assembly's Pastoral Letter to the People of Scotland on Family Worship.

———o———

EDINBURGH, *May* 30, 1836. *Sess. ult.*

THE GENERAL ASSEMBLY, having considered and approved the Overtures recommending a renewed Admonition for the purpose of stirring up the people of this land to the faithful and regular observance of the Worship of God in their Families, did, and hereby do, require the following PASTORAL LETTER to be read by all the Ministers of this Church from their several pulpits, on the first convenient Lord's Day after it shall come into their hands.

JOHN LEE, *Cl. Eccl. Scot.*

THE GENERAL ASSEMBLY of the CHURCH of SCOTLAND, To our dearly beloved people: Grace, mercy, and peace, from God the Father, and Christ Jesus our Lord.

On your behalf, brethren, we thank God, whom we serve with our spirit in the Gospel of His Son, that your faith and devotion have long been spoken of throughout the world; and we are bound always to have remembrance of you in our prayers night and day, greatly desiring that, like your forefathers in times of clearest light, you may continue steadfastly in the fear of the Lord, and in the comfort of the Holy Ghost, abounding in the exercises of that unfeigned godliness which is profitable unto all things, having promise of the life that now is and of that which is to come.

In compliance with the solicitations of many who watch for your souls, and are jealous over you with godly jealousy, we have resolved to issue this brotherly exhortation on the sacred and indispensable duty of Family Worship—not as if we had any recent ground for apprehending that it is likely to fall into more extensive neglect, but because we know too well that it is by no means universally practised, and because even the purest minds require to be stirred up by way of remembrance, that, while they hold fast the profession of their own faith without wavering, they may consider one another to provoke and encourage, by good counsel and good example, to the love of truth and holiness, and to the habitual and serious observance of those offices of piety, whereby, as surely as the body is nourished and refreshed by its daily bread and its nightly rest, the soul of man, through the nurture and admonition of the Lord, is progressively matured in excellence and strength, till it is advanced to the perfection and glory of its immortal existence.

In calling your attention to this momentous topic, we think it superfluous to enlarge on the high obligations by which the duty is enforced—obligations which are involved in the very constitution of our frail and dependent being, and impressed on the understanding and the heart by the persuasive voice of scriptural authority, opening the ears of men, and sealing the instruction by which God speaketh, not once or twice, but at sundry times, and in divers manners, adding line upon line, precept upon precept, promise upon promise, and threatening upon threatening, so as to bring perpetually to remembrance both the blessings which are multiplied to them that fear the Lord, and the fury which is poured out on the families which call not on His name. The appointment of the reasonable service of bowing down at the domestic altar before the Lord our Maker, that, in waiting for the promised effusion of the Spirit of grace and supplications, we may be filled with the fruits of righteousness, has ever been regarded by all men of sound mind and Christian experience, not as the imposition of an irksome yoke, but as the conveyance of an inestimable privilege; for as often as we mark the tokens of God's power and presence in making the outgoings of the morning and evening to rejoice, must every enlightened and purified heart, lifting up its affections to the Father of spirits, acknowledge, with triumphant satisfaction, that it is a good thing to show forth His loving-kindness in the morning and His faithfulness every night.

To those only who have tasted and seen it, can we speak intelligibly of the tranquil delight which is awakened and sustained by such periodical acts of household worship, as are not a mere formal ceremony in which the members join with reluctant or cold compliance, but the fervent utterance of lips which, out of the abundance of the heart in which the love of God is shed abroad, are, by the influence of that unquenchable affection, most pleasingly constrained to celebrate the mercies which are new every morning, and to offer up the spiritual incense of prayer with as unceasing regularity as from the sanctuary of Israel the smoke of the evening sacrifice arose, or as the early dew of Hermon descended on the mountains of Sion, when there the Lord commanded the blessing, even life for evermore.

Without all controversy, the benefits produced by this hallowed exercise are ineffably precious. It is not enough to say that thus are devout and grateful emotions awakened—thus is faith in the superintending providence and holy promises of God confirmed—thus are the graces of humility, resignation, and patience, nourished and increased—while with the contemplation of the infinite excellence, the unwearied beneficence, and the everlasting strength of the Lord Jehovah, we contrast the instability, deceitfulness, and desperate wickedness of the heart of man. By the infallible testimony of Heaven, we are authorised to affirm constantly that there is an efficacy in the prayer of faith, which, though inexplicable by our feeble understandings, must, through all ages, continue to avail as much as it did in the days of those patriarchs, prophets, and righteous men, who as princes had power with God, when, receiving a kingdom which cannot be moved, they had grace to serve Him acceptably with reverence and godly fear. The Lord is ever nigh unto them that are of a broken heart, and saveth such as be of a contrite spirit, when, taking with them the words which inspired wisdom has taught them to utter, they lift up their desires at His footstool, not seeking great things for themselves, or panting after the dust of the earth, or sighing for the vain delights of the sons of men, but thirsting and longing for the blessedness of the man whose transgression is forgiven, and who, being justified by faith, has peace with God through our Lord Jesus Christ. We have no encouragement to hope that, by taking thought for temporal satisfactions, we shall find grace in the sight of the Lord; but if we aspire after the best gifts which are the heritage of the faithful, seeking first the kingdom of God and His righteousness, we believe and are sure that His divine power will give us all things that pertain unto life and godliness, through the knowledge of Him that hath called us to glory and virtue. Though our Father in heaven knoweth what things we have need of before we ask them, and though the purposes of His everlasting kindness are often fulfilled more substantially by withholding than by granting the desires which we naturally cherish, it is only to them who worship Him in spirit and in truth that He has promised to do exceeding abundantly above all that they ask or think; and we have no more solid ground to expect that we shall receive without asking, or that we shall find without seeking, than the husbandman has to look for an abundant harvest springing up in the fields which he has neither planted nor watered, or than the merchant has to calculate on receiving his own with usury, for the talent which has been tied up in a napkin or buried in the earth.

It is not for us to unfold the laws of the spiritual world, or to demonstrate why and how it is that the communications of heavenly influence and favour are in any degree suspended on the frequency and fervency of our supplications. But this we know, that, as in old time the father of the faithful commanded his children, and his household after him, to unite with him in the exercises of a holy life, that the Lord might bring upon Abraham that which He had spoken of him,—even so, in all generations, may the willing and obedient hope that, while, seeking unto God and committing their cause to Him who doeth great things and unsearchable, they place their confidence not in their own importunity or their own efforts, but in the exalted merit and prevalent intercession of the Mediator of the New Covenant, they cannot fail to be made partakers of that abundant grace which ought to be the chief object of all our prayers, and which is never denied to the humble. We know assuredly that our heavenly Father giveth His Holy Spirit to them who ask Him; and if, for the sake of His beloved Son, He is pleased to bestow this unspeakable gift in answer to the prayer of the believing soul, why should we hesitate to admit that it is of the Lord's mercies that, by the eternal ordination of divine wisdom, prayer has been rendered one of the sure and sufficient means of transmitting to the faithful, every other good and perfect gift which cometh down from the Father of Lights, with whom is no variableness, neither shadow of turning?

To the duties of social prayer and thanksgiving, accompanied with that instruction in righteousness which the reading of the Scriptures is calculated to impart, let the benefits thus conferred on your several domestic circles operate as a strong incitement. It is not indeed within the compass of human ability to infuse grace into the souls which are most tenderly beloved. But great will probably be the influence of a pious example on those who confide in your affection, and have cause to revere your worth. If your children and dependants perceive that, while you are not slothful in the business of time, you are also fervent in spirit, serving the Lord, and that, while you provide for your own the food and the raiment which are obtained by the blessing of God on the hand of the diligent, you ask for them that bread of Heaven which strengtheneth the heart, may you not hope that they will be stirred up both to pray and to labour for the meat which endureth to life everlasting, and that they will learn to regard the favour of God as a better portion than the abundance of corn and wine? May you not hope that, while your own minds are elevated by contemplating the works of creation, providence, and redemption, and by reflecting on the dignified and endearing relation to which you have been raised in having "received the spirit of adoption, whereby you cry, Abba, Father," they who look up to you for guidance and protection will take pleasure in approaching to God, and, through the experience of the peace of walking with the wise, will be taught to abhor the enticements of sinners, and to hold fast that which is good? And even in the case of those who, through perversity of heart, and the snares of an evil world, have forsaken the path of integrity and truth, may it not be hoped that the wise counsels which they have for a season forgotten. and the devotional habits which they have long failed to imitate, will, like the bread cast upon the waters, be found after many days? Small must have been your experience of the discipline of Providence, if you have never known so much as one who had wandered so far from the way of peace as to disappoint the earnest expectations of his father, and to turn the joy of her who bare him into bitterness, but who, after his own wickedness had corrected him, and his backslidings reproved him, has been awakened to new obedience, by recalling to his agonised mind with reverential awe the solemn image of the parental guide, in whose quiet habitation the daily exercises of prayer and praise hallowed every pursuit, lightened every care, soothed every sorrow, and seasoned every enjoyment, so as to render the voice of rejoicing and salvation in the tabernacles of the righteous a lively type of the blessed conversation of heaven, and a delicious foretaste of the fellowship of the saints in light.

If ye know these things by your own experience, or by

the incontrovertible testimony of them who have tasted that the Lord is gracious, happy are ye if ye do them. Nor can you have peace and safety if, knowing what is good, you leave it undone.

And while you present your supplications for yourselves and your families, forget not the eternal concerns of the families which call not on the name of God. If it be, as it ought to be, your heart's desire that they may be brought to the obedience of the gospel, brethren, pray for us, and for all the ministers of the truth, that the word of the Lord may have free course and be glorified, even as it is with you. Such an intercession as this will assuredly prove efficacious towards the enlargement of the household of faith, if all of you, both small and great, not only in the congregations of the upright, who in heaviness of heart sigh for the abounding of iniquity, and the failing of truth, but in your families apart, and in your unseen retirements, prostrate yourselves at the footstool of your Father in heaven, who seeth in secret, and pour out your desires before Him in that effectual fervent importunity which, like the long and patient waiting of the husbandman for the precious fruit of the earth, will, according to the sure word of promise, issue in plenteous showers of blessings, not confined to any favoured spot, or any privileged community, but dropping down fertility far and wide over fields coextensive with the inhabited world, filled as it shall be in that evening time of light with the knowledge of the glory of the Lord, as the waters cover the sea: And thus the God of the whole earth, in remembrance of His holy covenant, and in fulfilment of the good pleasure of His goodness, will arise and have mercy not only on the mountain of holiness in which He had His dwelling in time past, but on all in every place who call on the name of Jesus Christ our Lord; so that, while

He clothes His priests with salvation, and makes His people shout for joy, the ways of Sion, which have mourned because few came to the solemn feasts, shall be thronged with the multitudes who keep the holy day with thanksgiving in their hearts, and the high praises of God in their mouths,—wisdom and knowledge shall be the stability of those times of refreshing from the presence of the Lord, when His work shall appear before the face of His servants and His glory to their children; and they that fear the Lord, being all replenished with the riches of grace, shall take that sweet counsel together which revives the inward part, and knits the brotherhood of Christians in the unity of the faith and the holy bond of perfectness. "Then shall the offering of His people be pleasant unto the Lord as in the days of old and as in former years." "And the Lord will create upon every dwelling-place of Mount Sion, and upon her assemblies, a cloud and smoke by day, and the shining of a flaming fire by night; for upon all the glory shall be a defence."

Finally, brethren, farewell. Be perfect; be of good comfort; be of one mind; live in peace; And the God of love and peace shall be with you.

The grace of the Lord Jesus Christ, and the love of God, and the communion of the Holy Ghost, be with you all.—Amen.

Prayers for Family Worship.

―――o―――

INTRODUCTORY PRAYERS.

One of these short Introductory Prayers may be used at the commencement of Family Worship, before the reading of a portion of Holy Scripture, after which may be used the longer Prayers.

I.

O GOD, who hast promised to be present with Thy people, and to grant their requests for whatsoever things they ask of Thee in the name of Thy beloved Son, regard us, we beseech Thee, with Thy favour, and graciously fulfil Thy promise in our behalf; that, offering up our desires unto Thee for things agreeable to Thy most blessed will, we may obtain our petitions through Jesus Christ our Lord.—Amen.

II.

O LORD our God, who art graciously inviting us to read Thy Word and to join together in Thy worship, be pleased to have compassion on our infirmities, and give us grace that we may profit by Thy teaching, and serve Thee acceptably with reverence and godly fear, through Jesus Christ our Lord.—Amen.

III.

ALMIGHTY GOD, our heavenly Father, who knowest what things we have need of before we ask, and art able to do exceeding abundantly above all that we ask or think, direct and aid us, we beseech Thee, in our supplications; that, though of ourselves we know not how to pray, and are not worthy that Thou shouldst grant our requests, we may ask and obtain whatsoever is expedient for us, according to Thy glorious riches in Christ Jesus; to whom, with Thee and with the Holy Spirit, be honour and praise for evermore.—Amen.

IV.

O GOD, who hast given Thy Word as a lamp to our feet and a light to our path, dispose us meekly to receive it, and enable us carefully to obey it, that, being upheld and guided in Thy ways, we may walk in holiness and in righteousness before Thee all the days of our life, and finally come to Thine everlasting kingdom, through Jesus Christ our Lord.—Amen.

V.

ALMIGHTY GOD, who inhabitest eternity, but dwellest also with the broken and contrite spirit, incline Thine ear to the voice of our supplications, and pour out upon us the grace of Thy Holy Spirit, that, humbled for our sins, and trembling at Thy Word, we may be revived and comforted with Thy fellowship, and may render unto Thee acceptable worship; through Jesus Christ our Lord.—Amen.

VI.

O LORD, without whom we can do nothing as we ought, assist us in our supplications which we make to Thee in the name of Thy beloved Son, and enlighten our minds in the knowledge of Thy truth, that the words of our mouth, and the meditation of our heart, may be acceptable in Thy sight, O God, our strength and our Redeemer.—Amen.

VII.

O GOD, who art a Spirit, and who wouldst be worshipped in spirit and in truth, give us, we beseech Thee, the dispositions of true worshippers, and let our humble endeavours in Thy service be aided by the grace of Thy Holy Spirit, and accepted through the mediation of Thy beloved Son, our Lord and only Saviour.—Amen.

VIII.

O GOD, by whose inspiration all Holy Scripture hath been written, grant that Thy Word may be profitable to us for doctrine, for reproof, for correction, and for instruction in righteousness, so as to make us wise unto salvation, and thoroughly furnished unto all good works, through Jesus Christ our Lord.—Amen.

IX.

GRACIOUS GOD, in whom alone dwelleth all fulness of light and wisdom, illuminate our minds, we beseech Thee, by Thy Holy Spirit, in the true understanding of Thy Word. Give us grace to receive it with reverence, and humility, and faith unfeigned. And enable us so faithfully to obey it, that by our godly lives we may edify our brethren, and glorify Thy holy name, through Jesus Christ our Lord.—Amen.

X.

O LORD, who hast deigned to instruct us by Thy heavenly doctrine, dispose us with meekness and humility to learn of Thee, and give us grace to profit by Thy teaching, through Jesus Christ our Lord.—Amen.

XI.

O THOU that hearest prayer, and canst alone teach us to pray to Thee as we ought, enable us with fixedness of mind and fervency of heart to call upon Thy name; and grant us the aid and guidance of Thy Holy Spirit, that we may ask such things as shall please Thee, through Jesus Christ our Lord.—Amen.

XII.

O GOD, who hast taught us to approach Thee as children to a Father able and ready to help us, send forth the Spirit of Thy Son into our hearts, that we may draw near unto Thee with all holy reverence and confidence, and may obtain the petitions which we ask of Thee, through Jesus Christ our Lord.—Amen.

XIII.

O GOD, who by the entrance of Thy words givest light unto the simple, fill us, we beseech Thee, with the knowledge of Thy will in all wisdom and spiritual understanding, that we may walk worthy of Thee unto all pleasing, and may be fruitful in every good work, through Jesus Christ our Lord.—Amen.

XIV.

O LORD, who hast taught us that if men, being evil, know how to give good gifts unto their children, much more shall our Father which is in heaven give good things to them that ask Him; enable us, with the confidence of Thy children, to spread out before Thee the desires of our hearts; and let it please Thee to supply all our need according to the fulness of Thy mercy in Christ Jesus, our Lord and only Mediator.—Amen.

XV.

O GOD, who hast promised to all who lack wisdom and ask it of Thee, that Thou wilt liberally give it, enlighten our minds, we beseech Thee, by Thy Word and Spirit, that we may no longer be children in understanding, but may grow up unto the stature of a perfect man, and be prepared for every good work, to the glory of Thy name, through Jesus Christ our Saviour.—Amen.

XVI.

O GOD, who hast encouraged us to approach Thee in the name of Thy beloved Son, who ever liveth to make intercession for us, make us thankful that we have not a High Priest who cannot be touched with the feeling of our infirmities; and enable us to come boldly unto the throne of grace, that we may obtain mercy, and find grace to help in time of need, through Jesus Christ our Lord.—Amen.

XVII.

O GOD, who hast taught us in the Scriptures what we are to believe concerning Thee, and what duty Thou requirest of us, open our hearts to receive meekly the engrafted Word which is able to make us wise unto salvation, through faith which is in Christ Jesus, to whom be glory for ever and ever.—Amen.

XVIII.

O GOD, who hast taught us to be careful for nothing, but in everything, by prayer and supplication, with thanksgiving, to make our requests known unto Thee; pour out upon us a spirit of grace and of supplications, and enable us so to cast our care upon Thee, that the peace of God which passeth all understanding may keep our hearts and minds through Christ Jesus, to whom, with Thee and with the Holy Spirit, be glory everlasting.—Amen.

XIX.

GRACIOUS GOD, who hast caused all Holy Scripture to be written for our learning, grant that Thy Word may come to us in power, and in the Holy Ghost, and in much assurance, and that we may receive it, not as the word of men, but, as it is in truth, the Word of God, which effectually worketh in them that believe, through Jesus Christ our Lord.—Amen.

XX.

O LORD, open Thou our lips, and our mouth shall show forth Thy praise. Pardon our unworthiness. Help our infirmities. And graciously receive the worship which we render to Thee, through Jesus Christ our Lord.—Amen.

XXI.

O LORD, who hast said that where two or three are gathered together in Thy name there art Thou in the midst of them, vouchsafe to us Thy presence and Thy blessing. Let Thy fear be upon us; let Thy grace be helpful to us; let Thy Word come to us in power and be received in love; and whatsoever we do, enable us to do it heartily, as to the Lord, and not unto men, through Jesus Christ our Saviour.—Amen.

XXII.

ALMIGHTY GOD, without whom we can do nothing, dispose us with humility to rely on the light of Thy Word and the grace of Thy Holy Spirit;

and grant that all our endeavours in Thy service may be acceptable to Thee and profitable to ourselves, through Jesus Christ our Lord.—Amen.

XXIII.

ALMIGHTY GOD, with whom are hid all the treasures of wisdom and knowledge, open our eyes that we may behold wondrous things out of Thy Law, and give us grace that we may clearly understand and heartily choose the way of Thy commandments, through Jesus Christ our Lord.—Amen.

XXIV.

O GOD, of whose grace alone it cometh that we are able to pray to Thee as we ought, deliver us, when we draw nigh to Thee, from wanderings of thought and coldness of affection, and enable us in faith to ask of Thee such things as it shall please Thee to bestow, through the merits of Jesus Christ, our only Mediator.—Amen.

XXV.

FOR THE LORD'S DAY.

ALMIGHTY GOD, Creator of heaven and earth, who wast pleased of old to hallow the seventh day, wherein Thou didst rest from all Thy works which Thou hadst made, grant that in this our Christian Sabbath we may cease from our own works, as Thou didst from Thine, and that when we have diligently laboured in Thy service all the days of our appointed time on earth, we may be partakers of the everlasting rest which remaineth for Thy people in heaven, through Jesus Christ our Lord.—Amen.

XXVI.

FOR THE LORD'S DAY.

ALMIGHTY GOD, Father of our Lord Jesus Christ, who didst, as on this day, raise up Thy Son from the dead and give Him glory, that our faith and hope might be in Thee, quicken us also, we beseech Thee, by Thy mighty power, from the death of sin to the life of righteousness, and cause us to set our affection on things above; so that we may at the last day have part in the resurrection of the just, and in the glory of Thy heavenly kingdom, whither Jesus the Forerunner is for us entered, where also He liveth and reigneth with Thee and the Holy Ghost, God blessed for ever.—Amen.

XXVII.

FOR THE LORD'S DAY.

O LORD our God, who hast commanded us to remember the Sabbath-day and keep it holy, enable us to sanctify the Sabbath by resting from the cares and pleasures of the world, and by giving up ourselves to Thy service. Teach us to call the Sabbath a delight, and grant us in the observance of it a foretaste of those heavenly joys which Thou wilt hereafter bestow upon Thy people, through Christ our Lord.—Amen.

XXVIII.

FOR THE LORD'S DAY.

O GOD of peace, who didst, as on this day, bring again from the dead our Lord Jesus, that great Shepherd of the sheep, through the blood of the everlasting covenant, make us perfect in every good work to do Thy will, working in us that which is pleasing in Thy sight, through Jesus Christ, to whom be glory for ever and ever.—Amen.

CONCLUDING PRAYERS.

The Lord's Prayer.

OUR Father which art in heaven, Hallowed be Thy name. Thy kingdom come. Thy will be done in earth, as it is in heaven. Give us this day our daily bread. And forgive us our debts, as we forgive our debtors. And lead us not into temptation, but deliver us from evil: For Thine is the kingdom, and the power, and the glory, for ever.—Amen.

The Blessing.

THE grace of the Lord Jesus Christ, and the love of God, and the communion of the Holy Ghost, be with us all.—Amen.

Prayers for Family Worship.

FIRST WEEK.

Lord's Day Morning.

O GOD, our Creator and Redeemer, who in Thy love to man hast set apart one day in seven to be a holy Sabbath, and in Thy merciful providence hast spared us to see another return of Thy sacred day, make us thankful for this precious season of rest and worship and instruction, and enable us by Thy grace to hallow it to those devout uses for which Thou hast appointed it.

We confess, O God, that we are prone to forget Thee amidst the pursuits and pleasures of the world. We acknowledge with shame that even on Thy holy day we have been inclined to follow our own ways, to speak our own words, and to find our own pleasure; and that often when we have come before Thee as Thy people come, and worshipped Thee with our lips, our hearts have been far from Thee.

Pardon, O God, for the sake of Thy beloved Son, our past aversion to Thy fellowship. Forgive the coldness and indifference we have shown to the honour of Thy name, and the sanctity of Thine ordinances. And now that Thou art again inviting us to remember the Sabbath-day and keep it holy, we humbly implore the grace of Thy Spirit to fit and prepare our hearts for the observance of it. Grant that we may be enabled this day to rest from our works as Thou didst from Thine, and to rise from worldly vanities and cares, as Christ our Lord was raised from the dead. Direct our thoughts to those things which belong to Thy glory and our own everlasting peace. And vouchsafe to us, in the keeping of Thine earthly Sabbath, a foretaste of that heavenly rest which Thou wilt hereafter bestow on Thy people.

Almighty God, who didst in the beginning command the light to shine out of darkness, shine, we beseech Thee, into our hearts, to give the light of the knowledge of Thy glory in the face of Jesus Christ our Saviour; and grant that, thus knowing Thee, we may heartily love Thee, and faithfully trust in Thee, and cheerfully obey Thee; and that, beholding with open face as in a glass the glory of the Lord, we may be changed into the same image from glory to glory, until, being fully conformed to Thy likeness, we are at length presented faultless before the presence of Thy glory with exceeding joy.

O God, who hast promised that in all places where Thou dost record Thy name, Thou wilt come unto Thy people and wilt bless them, vouchsafe to us, and to all our fellow-worshippers in every place, Thy presence and Thy blessing. Enable Thy ministering servants solemnly to guide the devotions of Thy Church, and faithfully to declare the truths of Thy Gospel. And grant that their ministrations may be effectual for the conversion of sinners, and for the building up of saints in holiness and comfort through faith unto salvation.

Be very gracious to those who are withheld by sickness, or any other necessary cause, from worshipping Thee in the assemblies of Thy people; and cause them to feel, in the privacy of their dwellings, that Thou art ever nigh to such as truly seek Thee.

Have pity on those who wilfully forsake Thine ordinances and profane Thy holy day. Convince them of their guilt, and bring them to repentance.

Increase everywhere the number of Thy true worshippers; and hasten the time when incense and a pure offering shall ascend unto Thee from the rising unto the setting sun.

To Thy special care and guidance we commit ourselves, and all who are near and dear to us, this day. O send out Thy light and Thy truth; let them lead us, and bring us to Thy tabernacles. Then will we go to the altar of God, unto God our exceeding joy. Cause us to feel that it is good for us to draw near to Thee. And let it please Thee, O God, to remember us with the favour that Thou bearest unto Thy people, and to visit us with Thy salvation.

Graciously hear us, for the sake of Thy beloved Son, to whom, with Thee, and with the Holy Spirit, be glory and majesty, dominion and blessing, world without end. —Amen.

Lord's Day Evening.

ALMIGHTY GOD, Father of mercies, from whom cometh down every good and perfect gift, we lift up our souls unto Thee in prayer and supplication with thanksgiving.

We thank Thee for the instructions of Thy Word, the rest of Thy Sabbath, the ordinances of Thy worship, and all our Christian privileges and means of grace; above all, for the promise of Thy Holy Spirit to bless them, and make them effectual for our salvation. We praise Thy name that we are more highly favoured than prophets and kings and righteous men of old, who desired to see the things which we see but saw them not, and to hear the things which we hear but heard them not; and that Thou hast greatly distinguished us above many of our fellow-creatures who are still sitting in gross darkness, by causing the Dayspring from on high to visit us, and guiding our feet into the way of life and peace.

Make us duly sensible, we beseech Thee, of the great and manifold advantages Thou hast conferred upon us. Enter not into judgment with Thy servants for the negligence, unfaithfulness, and sinfulness wherewith we have hitherto slighted or abused them. And help us, for the time to come, more justly to value our privileges, and with greater care and earnestness to improve them, that they may not at last rise against us to our condemnation.

Almighty God, who hast called us with a holy calling, not according to our works, but according to Thine own purpose and grace in Christ Jesus, and hast blessed us in Him with all spiritual blessings, grant that we may in everything be enriched by Him, so as to come behind in no gift. Perfect that which is lacking in our faith; make us to increase and abound more and more in love to Thee, and in charity to our fellow-men; cause us to be filled with the knowledge of Thy will in all wisdom and spiritual understanding, that we may walk worthy of the Lord unto all pleasing, being fruitful in every good work.

O Lord our God, who hast graciously promised an everlasting rest to Thy people hereafter, and hast given Thy Sabbath to foreshadow it, and to prepare us for it; help us with all diligence and faithfulness to labour that we may enter into that rest; and enable us so to profit by our use of the ordinances and instructions of Thy holy day, that, going on from strength to strength, we may every one of us appear in Zion before Thee, and may enjoy there the blessedness of those that dwell in Thy house and are for ever praising Thee.

We pray that everywhere, even as with us, Thy Word may have free course and be glorified; that Thy ministering servants may be faithful and successful; that Thy Church may be edified, purified, and extended; that the outcasts of Israel and the fulness of the Gentiles may be gathered into the fold of the great Shepherd and Bishop of souls; and that the blessed day may soon come when the knowledge of Thy Gospel shall cover the whole earth.

We pray for the welfare and happiness of our Sovereign; for the good of our country; for the peace of all nations.

We pray for the poor, the sick, the dying, and all who are in danger or distress; that it may please Thee to comfort and support them, and to give them a happy issue out of all their troubles.

[Bestow Thy blessing on the young of this family. Guide them in the ways of godliness; and satisfy them early with Thy mercy, that they may rejoice and be glad all their days. Regard with Thy favour the servants of this household, and enable them, by all good fidelity in their appointed station, to honour and serve Thee their great Master in heaven.]

To Thy fatherly care, O God, we commend ourselves, and all who are near and dear to us; beseeching Thee to defend us this night from all evil, and to bring us in safety to the light of a new day.

O Thou that hearest prayer, incline Thine ear to our humble supplications. Remember not against us our manifold transgressions, which render us unworthy of the least of Thy mercies. And do to us, not according to our imperfect asking, but according to Thine infinite goodness in Christ Jesus, to whom, with Thee, and with the Holy Spirit, be honour and praise for ever and ever. —Amen.

Monday Morning.

O GOD, our Creator and Preserver, who, by the rest of Thy holy Sabbath, and by the slumbers of the past night, hast restored our souls and refreshed our bodies, we thankfully acknowledge Thy goodness, and yield up ourselves anew to Thy service.

Suffer us not, we beseech Thee, when returning to the ordinary concerns of this life, to be forgetful of the instructions of Thy Word, or to cast off the hallowed influence of Thy worship. May every wholesome lesson be remembered, every good impression deepened, every holy resolution confirmed. Help us to carry the spirit of the Sabbath into the business of the week, so that, amidst all our labours, our souls may still rest in Thee, and that, whether we eat or drink, or whatsoever we do, we may do all to Thy glory.

We confess, O God, that our goodness has often been as the morning cloud or early dew, that passeth away. And we beseech Thee to pardon our unsteadfastness, and to give us grace, whereby we may be enabled more constantly and consistently to walk with Thee. Let the life we henceforth lead in the body be a life of faith in the Son of God, who loved us and gave Himself for us; and let our profiting by the grace He hath conferred appear in our habitual temper and conversation.

O Lord, without whom we can do nothing as we ought, help us in all our actions to maintain a strict regard to the precepts of Thy Word, and to abstain from all appearance of evil. Set a watch before our mouths, and keep the door of our lips, that no corrupt communications may proceed from them, but that which is good to the use of edifying. Cleanse our hearts from all unholy desires, from all worldly and covetous affections, from all malignant and uncharitable dispositions. And enable us so to manifest the power of godliness, that we may be living epistles of the Lord, known and read of all men.

Grant us this day Thy guidance and protection. Aid us in our appointed occupations. Support us in any trials or dangers that may befall us. Help us to endure as seeing Thee, who art invisible. And while we are diligent in seeking those things that are needful for our sustenance and comfort in the present world, make it to be our chief concern to lay up treasure in heaven, and to labour for the meat that endureth unto eternal life.

Let Thy blessing rest on the inmates of this dwelling. Give grace to all of us to discharge our several duties, as parents or children, masters or servants, with uprightness, fidelity, and diligence.

Bestow Thy favour on our relatives and friends. Prosper all the interests of our country. Bless our Sovereign, and all in authority over us, and dispose them ever to rule in Thy fear.

Provide for the poor; instruct the ignorant; reclaim the erring; pity the afflicted; impart relief and comfort to the sick; prepare for their great change those who are about to die.

We pray for all our brethren of mankind, that it may please Thee more and more widely to diffuse among them the knowledge of Thy saving truth, and to bring them to the faith and obedience of Thy Gospel.

Graciously hear our supplications, for the sake of Thy beloved Son, our Lord and Saviour.—Amen.

Monday Evening.

ALMIGHTY GOD, Father of our Lord Jesus Christ, of whom the whole family in heaven and earth is named, give us, we beseech Thee, the spirit of adoption, while we pour out before Thee the desires of our hearts; that, coming unto Thee with all holy confidence, as children to a father able and ready to help us, we may be accepted in the name of Thy beloved Son, and through Him receive the petitions which we ask of Thee.

Holy Father, we are unworthy to be called Thy children, because we have rebelled against Thee. We confess that we have been unthankful for Thy mercies, distrustful of Thy promises, and disobedient to Thy commandments; that we have despised Thy fatherly chastenings, and have turned a deaf ear to Thy counsels and reproofs; that we have kept back from Thee the affection of our hearts, and by our manifold wickedness have provoked Thee to cast us off from Thy fellowship and favour.

Merciful Father, grant us Thy forgiveness. Work in us true repentance towards Thee, and faith unfeigned towards the Lord Jesus Christ. And for His sake be merciful to our unrighteousness, and remember our iniquities no more.

Give unto us also Thy Holy Spirit, to witness with our spirits that we are Thy children, and to produce in us filial love, and trust, and gratitude, and obedience to Thy will. Make us kindly affectioned to our brethren, ready to bear with their errors and infirmities, and to do them good as we have opportunity. And amidst the toils and trials of our present condition, support and comfort us with the hope of that blessed inheritance which awaits us in our Father's kingdom.

O Thou bountiful Giver of all good, who knowest what things we have need of before we ask, and art able to do for us above all that we ask or think, we cast ourselves on Thy care, and plead with Thee, according to Thy promises, for all things truly necessary or expedient for us. Grant us, in all our duties, Thy help; in all our difficulties, Thy counsel; in all our trials and dangers, Thy protection; in all our sorrows, Thy peace and consolation. And whatsoever it may please Thee to give or to withhold, teach us to be contented with Thy will, and to rest with unshaken trust in Thine assurance, that all things work together for good to them that love Thee.

Father of mercies, whose power hath sustained us, whose bounty hath provided for us, whose love hath redeemed us, we render praise and thanksgiving unto Thee; acknowledging that we are not worthy of the least of all Thy benefits, and beseeching Thee so to impress them on our hearts, that we may be led to show our gratitude by a cheerful and steadfast obedience to Thy commandments.

We pray for all our relatives and friends, that they may be blessed with Thy favour and protection. We pray for those who are visited with affliction, that it may please Thee to comfort and relieve them.

Look with compassion on the whole human race. Promote their peace, their liberty, their happiness. Above all, bring them to the knowledge of Thy truth.

And now, O God, we commit ourselves to Thee. Grant us quiet sleep, and mercifully spare us to enjoy the blessings and discharge the duties of another day.

Graciously hear us, for the sake of Thy beloved Son, our Lord and Saviour.—Amen.

Tuesday Morning.

ALMIGHTY GOD, our Father and Preserver, we give Thee thanks that of Thy goodness Thou hast watched over us during the past night, and brought us to see the light of another day. Strengthen and guard us by Thy grace, we beseech Thee, that we may spend this day wholly in Thy service, seeking Thy glory and the good of our fellow-men. And even as Thou now sheddest the beams of the sun upon the earth to give light unto our bodies, let it please Thee also to illuminate our souls with the brightness of Thy Holy Spirit, that we may be guided in the paths of righteousness. Cause us to hear Thy loving-kindness in the morning, for in Thee do we trust. Cause us to know the way wherein we should walk; for we lift up our souls unto Thee.

We confess, O God, that by reason of our manifold sins we are unworthy to seek any blessing at Thy hands; but we beseech Thee, for the sake of Thy beloved Son, to blot out, as a thick cloud, our transgressions. Let them no longer stand between us and Thee, hiding from us the light of Thy countenance, and threatening us with the tempest of Thy wrath. But may it please Thee to cast them out of Thy remembrance, and of Thy boundless mercy to forgive them, as Thou hast promised unto such as call on Thee in truth.

Help us also for the time to come to yield up ourselves entirely to Thy service. Let it be the purpose of our whole lives to honour Thee. Teach us to look for all prosperity to Thy favour and blessing, and to seek only such things as are pleasing in Thy sight.

Assist us in the duties of our calling. Grant that while we are not slothful in business, we may also be fervent in spirit, serving the Lord. And enable us, while labouring for the life that now is, to look ever beyond it to that heavenly life which Thou hast promised to Thy children.

Defend us, O God, in soul and body, from all evil. Guard us against the assaults of the devil, the snares of the world, and the sinful desires of our own hearts. And seeing it is a small thing to have begun well, except we also persevere, take us, O Lord, into Thy good keeping this day and all our days. Continue and increase Thy grace within us, until we be perfected in the glory of our Lord Jesus Christ, the Sun of righteousness, who shall replenish our souls with His eternal light and gladness.

We pray for all our relatives and friends [especially for the young of this family], that Thou wouldst enrich them with the treasures of Thy grace.

We pray for the poor, the sick, the dying, and all who are in adversity or affliction, that it may please Thee to comfort and relieve them.

Extend Thy compassion, we beseech Thee, to all mankind. Put an end to war and discord, as well as to vice and superstition, everywhere. And speedily diffuse Thy Gospel throughout the earth, to enlighten and convert the nations that sit in darkness.

Graciously hear our humble supplications, according to the riches of Thy mercy in Jesus Christ, our Lord and only Saviour.—Amen.

Tuesday Evening.

O GOD, who hast appointed the night for rest and the day for labour, grant, we beseech Thee, that we may so rest in peace and quietness during the coming night, that afterwards we may be able to bear our appointed labours. Take us into Thy holy protection, so that no evil may befall us, and no plague may come nigh our dwelling. And although we have not passed this day without greatly sinning against Thee, yet let it please Thee, for the sake of Thy beloved Son, to hide our sins with Thy mercy, as Thou coverest all things on earth with the darkness of the night, and to bury them evermore out of Thy remembrance; that as our bodies are refreshed by quiet sleep, so also our minds may be made tranquil by a comfortable sense of Thy forgiveness.

We thank Thee, O God, that Thou hast not appointed us to wrath, but to obtain salvation by our Lord Jesus Christ, who died for us, that whether we wake or sleep, we should live together with Him. Help us, we pray Thee, with true faith to rest on Him, and all our life long with purpose of heart to cleave to Him. And when at length our days are ended, and our work is finished in this world, grant that we may depart hence in the blessed assurance of Thy favour, and in the sure hope of that glorious kingdom, where there is day without night, and life without the shadow of death, for ever.

We pray for Thy blessing on all our beloved friends. Guard them from evil by night and by day. Supply all their wants according to Thy glorious riches. Above all, enrich them with spiritual and heavenly blessings.

[Regard with Thy favour the children of this family. Deliver them from all the temptations that surround them, and cause them to grow in knowledge and in grace.

May the servants of this house remember that they have a Master in heaven, and find their appointed toils dignified and sweetened to them, by the thought that in all things they are serving the Lord Christ.]

We implore Thy blessing on the widow and the orphan, the poor, the sick, the sorrowful, and the dying. Succour and relieve them according to their necessities; and overrule Thy dealings with them for their spiritual good.

Bestow Thy favour on the British Empire and all its Colonies. Preserve to us our liberties and privileges. Bless our Sovereign and all in authority; enable them to rule in Thy fear; and grant that under them all orders of the people may lead quiet lives in godliness and honesty.

O God, who hast made of one blood all nations, and wouldst have all men to come to the knowledge of the truth, open, we beseech Thee, a great door and effectual for the preaching of Thy blessed Gospel everywhere; and hasten the time when all the ends of the earth shall turn to Thee, and all the kindreds of the nations shall worship before Thee.

And now, O Lord our God, we entreat Thee, incline Thine ear to the voice of our supplications; for we do not present them unto Thee for our own righteousnesses, but for Thy great mercies, and in the name of Thy beloved Son, our Lord and Saviour.—Amen.

Wednesday Morning.

ALMIGHTY and most merciful Father, it is a good thing to give thanks unto Thee, to sing praises unto Thy name, O Thou Most High, to show forth Thy loving-kindness in the morning, and Thy faithfulness every night. For in Thee we live, and move, and have our being; and from Thee cometh down every good and perfect gift.

We give unto Thee the glory that is due for having created us after Thine own image, and endowed us with the gifts of reason and of conscience, whereby we are capable of knowing and of serving Thee.

We thank Thee for the bounties of Thy providence; for health and strength; food and raiment; for manifold social blessings and domestic comforts; for seasonable help and succour in our times of need; for tender pity and consolation in our hours of sorrow; and for all the care and kindness Thou hast shown to us from our earliest infancy even until now.

Above all, we magnify Thy name for Thine unspeakable mercy to our souls. We thank Thee, that Thou hast given Thy beloved Son to be the propitiation for our sins; that Thou hast promised Thy Holy Spirit to sanctify our corrupt nature; that Thou hast called us out of darkness into the marvellous light of Thy Gospel; that Thou hast abundantly favoured us with means of grace, and hast comforted us with the hope of immortal glory.

Holy Father, let not our manifold sins, which have made us unworthy of the least of all Thy mercies, prevail with Thee to remove Thy blessings from us. Have mercy on us after Thy loving-kindness; according to the multitude of Thy tender mercies, blot out our transgressions. And for the sake of Thy beloved Son, in whom we have redemption through His blood, continue to us the tokens of Thy love, and visit us with the joy of Thy salvation.

Help us, we beseech Thee, for the time to come, more worthily to acknowledge Thy goodness. May we show our sense of it by unfeigned trust in Thee, by full contentment with the portion Thou hast given us, by kind and charitable dispositions towards our fellow-men, and by cheerful obedience to Thy holy commandments.

O God, by whose good hand upon us we have been spared to see the light of another day, and in whose merciful providence we are now called to go forth to our work and labour until the evening, grant us, in all our occupations, we beseech Thee, the aid of Thy strength, and the guidance of Thy wisdom. Teach us in all our ways to acknowledge Thee. And whatsoever we do, in word or in deed, enable us to do all in the name of the Lord Jesus, giving thanks to God even the Father by Him.

Graciously hear us, O God, while we plead with Thee for all whom we ought to remember at a throne of grace.

Bestow Thy favour on our relatives and friends. Reward with Thy bounty all that have done us good. Pardon and convert all who have done or wished us evil, and enable us to forgive them from the heart.

[We earnestly pray for the young members of this family, that they may be kept from the evil that is in the world, and taught to walk in the way of Thy commandments.

Give to the servants of this household, we beseech Thee, the grace that is needful for serving Thee, their heavenly Master, in the station which Thy providence hath assigned to them: And grant that whatsoever they do, they may do it heartily, as unto the Lord and not unto man.]

God of all comfort, have pity on the afflicted. Grant them Thy grace to sustain them in their hour of trial. And let Thy chastening, though for the present grievous, yield in them afterward the peaceful fruits of righteousness.

Look with compassion, we beseech Thee, on the whole world. Hasten the time when repentance and remission of sins shall be preached in the name of Jesus to all nations; and grant that wherever Thy Gospel is already known, its holy and blessed fruits may be more and more abundant.

Incline Thine ear, O God, to our supplications, and favourably receive the tribute of our praises, for the sake of Thy beloved Son, our Saviour; to whom, with Thee and with the Holy Ghost, be ascribed all glory, thanksgiving, and dominion, world without end.—Amen.

Wednesday Evening.

O GOD, who by Thy merciful providence hast guided and upheld us throughout the past day, and under whose watchful guardianship we are encouraged to lay ourselves down and sleep in peace during the coming night; we acknowledge our dependence on Thy care, and lift up our souls in thanksgiving for Thy goodness. Blessed be Thou, who daily loadest us with benefits, O God of our salvation.

Pardon, we beseech Thee, for the sake of Thy beloved Son, our past ingratitude for Thy manifold loving-kindnesses. Remember no more against us our transgressions, whereby we have provoked Thy just anger. Continue to us, notwithstanding our unworthiness, those temporal and spiritual blessings which hitherto we have received at Thy most bountiful hands. And teach us henceforth to show our thankfulness for them, by giving up ourselves to Thy service, and doing those things that are pleasing in Thy sight. O that there were such an heart in us, that we would fear Thee, and keep all Thy commandments always, that it might be well with us and with our children for ever.

Grant, O God, that our experience of Thy goodness may lead us, at all times, to put our trust in Thee. Cause us to feel assured that Thou, who hast blessed us hitherto, wilt bless us still, and wilt withhold from us nothing which Thou knowest, in Thine unerring wisdom, to be needful or expedient for us.

Grant also, that a due sense of Thine unmerited kindness may subdue in us every feeling of discontentment. May we meekly submit to our hardships or deprivations, acknowledging that they are unworthy to be compared with the bounties of Thy providence, and the riches of Thy grace.

Father of mercies, who doest good continually, and art kind even to the unthankful and the evil; teach us, in imitation of Thy beneficence, to be generous and compassionate towards our fellow-men, to bless them that curse us, and do good to them that hate us, to walk in love as Thou hast loved us, and from the heart to forgive one another, even as Thou for Christ's sake forgivest us.

God of all grace, we beseech Thee to extend to others the blessings and privileges with which we have ourselves been favoured. Have mercy on all our brethren of mankind, and bring them to the knowledge and reception of Thy truth. Further the cause of pure religion in our native land; and grant that we may be distinguished by that righteousness which exalteth a nation.

We pray for the sons and daughters of affliction, that it may please Thee to comfort and relieve them, and to overrule Thy fatherly chastening to the everlasting welfare of their souls.

And now, O God, we commit ourselves to Thee. Watch over us during the darkness of the night. Save us from all dangers. Grant us refreshing sleep; and bring us in peace to the light of a new day.

Graciously hear us, O Father, and have mercy on us, for the sake of Thy beloved Son, our strength and our Redeemer.—Amen.

Thursday Morning.

O LORD, who hast searched us and known us, who compassest our path and our lying down, and art acquainted with all our ways, we worship Thee as the ever-present God, who, though unseen, art not far from any one of us. Whither shall we go from Thy Spirit? or whither shall we flee from Thy presence? If we ascend up into heaven, Thou art there; if we make our bed in hell, behold Thou art there; if we take the wings of the morning, and dwell in the uttermost parts of the sea, even there shall Thy hand lead us, and Thy right hand shall hold us. If we say, Surely the darkness shall cover us, even the night shall be light about us. Yea, the darkness hideth not from Thee; but the night shineth as the day: the darkness and the light are both alike to Thee.

O God, who hast set our iniquities before Thee, and our secret sins in the light of Thy countenance, we humble ourselves in Thy most holy presence, acknowledging our utter unworthiness in Thy sight. O our God, we have cause to be ashamed before Thee, when we consider how little we have thought upon Thee; how often we have disregarded or forgotten Thee; how prone we have been to live without Thee in the world; how much Thou hast witnessed, in the ungodliness of our hearts and the sinfulness of our lives, that is hateful and offensive to Thee.

Enter not, O God, into judgment with Thy servants, for in Thy sight shall no man living be justified. But for the sake of Jesus Christ, who bore our sins in His own body on the cross, and ever liveth to make intercession for us, bestow upon us Thy forgiveness, and make the light of Thy countenance to shine upon us.

Give us grace also, whereby we may be enabled more faithfully to live as in Thy presence. Teach us in times of danger or of trouble to look up to Thee as our very present help. Dispose us in times of trial or temptation to stand in awe, lest in anything we offend Thee, who searchest our hearts, and triest our reins, and understandest our thoughts afar off. In all the concerns and occupations of our daily life, help us to endure as seeing Thee who art invisible. And when our course on earth is finished, grant, O God, that we may be supported and comforted with Thy presence in the valley of the shadow of death, and may at last come to the glories of Thy heavenly kingdom, and there be made perfectly blessed in seeing, serving, and enjoying Thee for ever.

O God, who wouldst have all men to come to the knowledge of the truth, send forth everywhere the light of Thy glorious Gospel; remove the veil from the hearts of Thine ancient people; dispel the darkness and superstition of the heathen; and hasten the time when all nations shall be blessed in Jesus, and shall call Him blessed.

We pray for Thy servants, who in every place make manifest the savour of Thy knowledge, that it may please Thee to strengthen and encourage them, and to make them faithful and successful in their great work.

Deal favourably, O God, with the land in which we dwell, and bless it with peace, and plenty, and prosperity. Be very gracious to our Sovereign the Queen. Defend her by Thy power; counsel her with Thy wisdom; and let her throne be established in righteousness.

Bestow Thy blessing, we beseech Thee, on our friends and kindred. Keep them from the evil that is in the world. Remember them for good, and visit them with Thy salvation.

Father of mercies, have pity on the afflicted. Relieve their distresses; assuage their griefs; and grant them a happy issue out of all their troubles.

Prepare us, O God, for every trial and for every duty As our day is, so let our strength be. Guide us by Thy counsel while we live, and afterward receive us into glory, for the Lord Jesus' sake.—Amen.

Thursday Evening.

O LORD our God, most high and most holy, who humblest Thyself to behold the things that are on earth, and dost not despise the supplication of the penitent; have mercy on us, Thine unworthy children, and favourably regard us for the sake of Thy beloved Son, through whom alone we have access to Thy throne of grace.

We acknowledge that in ourselves we are not worthy to lift up our eyes to heaven, or to take Thy holy name into our lips. We confess that our sins have been many and great, and that we are every day adding to their number. We have no cloak to hide them, and no plea to excuse them. Our own hearts condemn us on account of them; and Thou art greater than our hearts, and knowest all things.

Lord God, merciful and gracious, remember not against us, we beseech Thee, the sins of the past day, or of our past lives. Pardon whatever proud or vain thoughts we have harboured within us; whatever impatience and fretfulness we have betrayed; whatever worldliness of spirit we have cherished; whatever we have said or done that is inconsistent with supreme love to Thee, or fervent charity towards our brethren. Justify us freely by Thy grace through the redemption that is in Christ Jesus; and grant us, for His sake, the blessedness of the man whose transgression is forgiven, whose sin is covered, and unto whom Thou imputest not iniquity.

Gracious God, who desirest not sacrifice, and hast no delight in burnt-offering, but requirest of us to do justly, to love mercy, and to walk humbly with Thee; grant us, we pray Thee, the grace of true repentance; and so direct and govern our hearts and lives, that henceforth we may walk in the way of Thy commandments, and may offer unto Thee sacrifices of righteousness, well-pleasing in Thy sight, through Jesus Christ our Saviour.

Teach us every day to examine and prove ourselves in the light of Thy Holy Word, that we may not be continuing in any sin, or neglecting any duty. And let our rejoicing be the testimony of our conscience, that in simplicity and godly sincerity, not with fleshly wisdom, but by the grace of God, we have our conversation in the world.

O God, who art daily bearing with our sins, and crowning us with Thy loving-kindnesses, give unto us hearts more sensible of Thy love to us, and more full of love to Thee, and dispose us ever to seek our happiness in the enjoyment of Thy favour, the doing of Thy will, and the hope of Thy heavenly kingdom.

[Merciful Father, who givest Thy beloved sleep, let our rest this night be quiet and refreshing; and if it please Thee to raise us to another day, enable us faithfully to spend it in Thy service.]

We commend to Thy care our relatives and friends, beseeching Thee to remember them with the favour that Thou bearest unto Thy people, and to visit them with Thy salvation.

[We implore Thy blessing on the children of this family. Preserve them from the sins and dangers of youth. Incline their hearts to seek Thee early; and prepare them for serving Thee here and hereafter. Bestow Thy favour on the servants of this household. May they be faithful servants of the Lord Christ, and at last receive of Him the reward of the inheritance.]

Father of mercies and God of all comfort, have pity on those whom Thou hast visited with affliction, and let Thy chastening, though for the present grievous, yield in them afterward the peaceable fruits of righteousness.

Look with compassion, we beseech Thee, on our fellow-men who are sitting in gross darkness and perishing for lack of knowledge, cause Thy marvellous light to shine upon them; and hasten the time when all the nations of the earth shall be brought to the faith and obedience of Thy Gospel.

Give ear, O God, to our humble supplications, and grant unto us an answer of peace, for the Lord Jesus' sake.—Amen.

Friday Morning.

O GOD, through whose watchful providence we have slept in peace and awaked in safety, and to whose bounty we are indebted for the manifold comforts and blessings which surround us; we give Thee thanks for all Thy past goodness, and humbly implore Thy continued favour and protection. Thou art our God, early will we seek Thee. Our voice shalt Thou hear in the morning, O Lord; in the morning will we direct our prayer to Thee, and will look up.

We confess before Thee that we are fallen and sinful creatures, unworthy to receive any blessing at Thy hands. But we put our trust in Thy well-beloved Son, who gave Himself as a sacrifice for our sins, and ever liveth to make intercession for us. And in His name we earnestly beseech Thee to grant us Thy pardon, to aid us with Thy grace, to sanctify our souls for Thy service, and to supply all our need according to Thy glorious riches by Christ Jesus.

O God, who hast appointed to every man his proper work, and art now calling us, in the morning of another day, to go forth to our several occupations until the evening; teach us in all our ways to acknowledge Thee. Enable us to perform our allotted tasks with diligence, and to guide our affairs with prudence and discretion. And let it please Thee, in all our undertakings, to encourage us with Thy favour, to further us with Thy help, and to grant us such success as seemeth good to Thee, who orderest all things well and wisely for us.

Teach us, in our intercourse with our fellow-men, to walk in truth and uprightness before Thee; rendering unto all their dues, and doing unto others as we would that they should do to us. Dispose us, as much as lieth in us, to live peaceably with all men. Make us to be kindly affectioned one to another, ready to bear with the infirmities of the weak, to relieve the destitute, to comfort the afflicted, to reclaim the erring, to forgive the injurious, and to do good to all as we have opportunity.

Give us grace also, whereby we may be enabled to keep ourselves unspotted from the world. Suffer us not to be burdened with its cares, ensnared by its pleasures, corrupted by its riches, or led astray by its fashions and examples. Teach us to live above it and to look beyond it, confessing ourselves to be strangers on the earth, and desiring a better country, that is, a heavenly.

O Lord, who hast promised to such as seek first the kingdom of God and His righteousness, that all other needful things shall be added to them, enable us to put our trust in Thee, and grant us such deliverance, we beseech Thee, from anxious thoughts and covetous affections, that the peace of God which passeth understanding may keep our hearts and minds through Christ Jesus.

Father of mercies, extend Thy compassion to those who are disabled by sickness and infirmity for engaging in the active business of this life. Help them to glorify Thee in their affliction by a meek and patient submission to Thy will, and by a firm trust in Thy gracious promise, that all things work together for good to them that love Thee.

Bestow Thy favour on our friends and kindred. Deliver them from the evil that is in the world, and keep them by Thy power through faith unto salvation.

Bless all ranks and conditions of men among us.

Help them in their several stations faithfully to walk with Thee, and to lead quiet lives in godliness and honesty.

[O God, who blessest the springing of the earth, and crownest the year with Thy goodness, vouchsafe unto us favourable weather and fruitful seasons, that our pastures may be clothed with flocks, and our valleys covered with corn, and our souls may have cause to rejoice and be glad in Thee.]

Extend Thy mercy to all our brethren of mankind. Our heart's desire and prayer is that they may be saved. Let the people praise Thee, O God; let all the people praise Thee.

Grant these requests, O Father, we beseech Thee, and all other things which Thou knowest to be needful for us, according to Thy promises made to us in Jesus Christ, through whom we humbly offer our prayers, and to whom, with Thee and with the Holy Spirit, be glory everlasting.—Amen.

Friday Evening.

O LORD, who art good, and ready to forgive, and plenteous in mercy unto all them that call upon Thee; incline Thine ear, we beseech Thee, to our supplications, which we offer in the name of Thy well-beloved Son. Let our prayer be set forth before Thee as incense, and the lifting up of our hands as the evening sacrifice.

We thank Thee for the help and countenance Thou hast given us throughout the past day in our several occupations, and humbly beseech Thee to grant us, during the coming night, such quiet rest as shall enable us on the morrow to go forth again with renewed strength to our appointed labours.

Pardon, O God, wherein we have offended Thee by an undue concern for the things of the present world. We confess that we are apt to be engrossed with the cares and business and pleasures of this life; that we often suffer the vanities of earth to rob Thee of our homage and affection; and that, in the eagerness of our pursuit of things temporal, we are prone to forget or neglect those which are eternal.

O God, who knowest this our foolishness, grant us, for Christ's sake, Thy mercy to forgive it, and Thy grace effectually to restrain and turn us from it. Quicken our souls, that they cleave not to the dust. Convince us of the vanity of this world, and of its insufficiency to make us truly happy. Lead us to choose Thee, in preference to all Thy creatures, as our only sure and satisfying portion. Teach us to esteem Thy loving-kindness as better than life, and Thy law as more precious than thousands of gold and silver. And give us such views of the great and glorious things which Thou hast prepared for them that love Thee, as shall withdraw our affections from the world, and fix them on the joys and glories of Thy heavenly kingdom.

Blessed be Thou, O God and Father of our Lord Jesus Christ, who, according to Thine abundant mercy, hast begotten us again to a lively hope by the resurrection of Jesus Christ from the dead; to an inheritance incorruptible, and undefiled, and that fadeth not away, reserved for us in heaven. Grant, we beseech Thee, that, having this hope in us, we may be led by Thy grace to walk worthy of it. May we be crucified unto the world, and raised with Christ to newness of life. As risen with Him, enable us also in heart and mind to ascend with Him to heavenly places, and to seek those things which are above, where Christ sitteth at Thy right hand. And grant that, having our conversation in heaven, and our life hid with Christ in God, we may rest in the cheerful and confident persuasion, that when He who is our life shall appear, we also shall appear with Him in glory.

Graciously hear us, O God, while we plead with Thee, not for ourselves only, but also for our brethren. Cause Thy light to shine on those who are in darkness. Bring into the way of truth all who are deceived. Succour the tempted. Raise up the fallen. Provide for the destitute. Comfort the afflicted. Support the dying, and prepare them for their change.

And now, O God, we humbly commit ourselves and all who are near and dear to us, to thy care. Be merciful to us, we beseech Thee, and bless us, and make Thy face to shine upon us, for the Lord Jesus' sake.—Amen.

Saturday Morning.

O LORD our God, who dwellest on high, and art worshipped by unnumbered hosts of glorious spirits, that cease not to render to Thee pure and perfect homage; look down on us, Thy fallen and sinful creatures, from heaven the habitation of Thy holiness, and hearken to the voice of our prayers.

Remember not, we beseech Thee, our manifold offences, by reason of which we are unworthy to lift up our eyes to the place where Thine honour dwelleth. Graciously forgive us, for the sake of Thy beloved Son, who is the propitiation for our sins. And through Him let it please Thee to bestow upon us the grace of Thy Holy Spirit, whereby we may be disposed and enabled truly to love Thee, heartily to trust in Thee, and wholly to give up ourselves to Thy service.

O Lord, who hast called us to be holy as Thou art holy, and who canst alone make us such as Thou wouldst have us to be, fulfil in us all the good pleasure of Thy goodness, and stablish us in every good work, that we may stand perfect and complete in all Thy will. Create in us a clean heart, O God, and renew a right spirit within us. Enable us to put off the old man, which is corrupt according to the deceitful lusts, and, being renewed in the spirit of our minds, to put on the new man, which after God is created in righteousness and true holiness. Deliver us from evil thoughts, unholy passions, and uncharitable tempers; from pride and vanity, from malice and revenge, from envy and discontent, from covetousness and worldliness. Cause us to abound more and more in faith, and love, and temperance, and godliness;

in all holy desires; in all good purposes; in all kind and brotherly affections; in all meek, patient, humble, sober, pure, and peaceable dispositions: that the name of our Lord Jesus Christ may be glorified in us and we in Him, according to the grace which through Him Thou hast bestowed upon us. O God of peace, sanctify us wholly. And grant that our whole spirit, and soul, and body, may be established in holiness before Thee, and preserved blameless, unto the coming of our Lord Jesus Christ with all His saints.

Graciously hear us, O God, while we plead with Thee for all whom we ought to remember in our prayers. We commend our friends to Thy favour, our benefactors to Thy bounty, our enemies to Thy forgiveness.

[We pray for the children of this family, that they may be trained up in Thy fear: and for the servants, that they may be enabled to show all good fidelity in their appointed station.]

We beseech Thee to look with compassion on the afflicted, and to grant them all needful consolation and relief. We pray for the dying, that it may please Thee to comfort and sustain them, when flesh and heart are failing. We pray for all men, that Thou wouldst enlighten and convert them, until the whole world be filled with Thy glory.

And now, O God, we commit ourselves to Thee. Assist us this day in our several occupations. And whatsoever we do, in word or deed, enable us to do all in the name of the Lord Jesus; through whom we humbly offer our prayers, and to whom, with Thee and with the Holy Spirit, be all honour and glory, for evermore.—Amen.

Saturday Evening.

HEAVENLY FATHER, who hast safely brought us to the close of another day and of another week, help us to look back with gratitude on all the way by which Thou hast led us, and on all the care and kindness Thou hast shown towards us. Make us truly thankful, we beseech Thee, for the preservation of our lives and the supply of our daily wants; for health of body and soundness of mind; for the comforts of domestic peace and social intercourse; for strength and skill to labour in our callings, and for whatever success our labours may have attained;—above all, for Thine unwearied patience in bearing with our oft-repeated sins and provocations, and Thine unspeakable mercy in continuing to us the means of grace and the hope of glory.

O Lord our God, who art long-suffering and full of compassion; who waitest to be gracious, and willest not the death of a sinner, but rather that he should turn to Thee and live; grant that Thy goodness may lead us to repentance. Humble us while we think of all the evil we have done, and of all the good we have omitted in the days that are past. Teach us to reflect, with godly sorrow and contrition of heart, on the time we have wasted, the talents we have abused, the privileges and opportunities we have neglected; on all our past ingratitude for Thy goodness, and distrust of Thy promises, and disobedience to Thy commandments. Help us, under a deep conviction of our sinfulness, to put our trust in Thy well-beloved Son, in whom alone we have redemption through His blood. And for His sake let it please Thee to bestow upon us the pardon of our manifold offences, and the promised grace of Thy Holy Spirit; that, being restored to the enjoyment of Thy favour, and renewed in holiness after Thine image, we may bring forth fruits meet for repentance, and live to the praise and glory of Thy name.

O God, who hast made our days as an handbreadth, so that our age is as nothing before Thee, impress us with a sense of our frailty. So teach us to number our days that we may apply our hearts unto wisdom; and while week after week is swiftly gliding away, dispose us to walk circumspectly, redeeming the time, and to give heed to the things which belong unto our peace before they are hid from our eyes. Let the darkness and silence of the coming night admonish us of the time when we shall be laid upon a bed of death, and carried to the place appointed for all living. And lest that time should come upon us unawares, before the great business of life hath been accomplished, teach us to be sober, watchful, and prayerful; and to do with all our might whatsoever our hand findeth, for the advancement of Thy glory, the good of our fellow-men, and the furtherance of our own spiritual welfare; and grant that after having done and suffered Thy will upon the earth, we may depart in peace, and may have an entrance ministered to us abundantly into the everlasting kingdom of our Lord and Saviour Jesus Christ.

To Thy fatherly care, O God, we commit ourselves, and all who are near and dear to us, this night. Grant us refreshing sleep under the shadow of Thy wings; and, if it please Thee, spare us in Thy good providence to see the light of Thy holy day, and fit us for the profitable discharge of its solemn duties.

Hear our intercessions, we beseech Thee, for those whom we ought to remember at a throne of grace. Bless our rulers, counsellors, and pastors, and all who are in offices of trust and of authority, and aid them with Thy grace in the work Thou hast assigned to them. Bestow Thy favour on our relatives and friends. Protect them by Thy power; guide them by Thy counsel; and visit them with Thy salvation.

Look down in pity on the sick and the afflicted; comfort and relieve them according to their necessities; and overrule Thy chastening for their eternal good.

Have mercy on all the family of mankind. Diffuse among them the knowledge of Thy Gospel, and bring them to a saving reception of its grace and truth.

These, our humble supplications, we present before Thee, O Thou that hearest prayer. Graciously answer them, for the sake of Jesus Christ, to whom, with Thee and with the Holy Spirit, be honour and glory, for evermore.—Amen.

SECOND WEEK.

Lord's Day Morning.

ALMIGHTY and most merciful God, who art nigh to all that call on Thee in truth; incline Thine ear, we beseech Thee, to our supplications, and graciously receive the tribute of our praise. Keep us mindful that Thou wilt be sanctified in them that come nigh unto Thee, and that before all the people Thou wilt be glorified. And give us grace, whereby we may be enabled to serve Thee acceptably, with reverence and godly fear.

Thou art worthy, O God, to receive blessing, and honour, and thanksgiving. Thy power hath created us; Thy bounty hath sustained us; Thy patience hath spared us; Thy love hath redeemed us. Blessed be Thou, who daily loadest us with benefits, O God of our salvation.

We confess, O Lord, that we are unworthy to approach Thee, by reason of our manifold offences. For we have been foolish, disobedient, and deceived; we have loved the creature more than the Creator; we have sought the pleasures of earth more than the joys of heaven; we have walked according to the course of this world, fulfilling the desires of our own evil hearts.

O God, who knowest all our foolishness, and from whom our sins are not hid, have mercy upon us after Thy loving-kindness; and, according to the multitude of Thy tender mercies, blot out our transgressions. Forgive us all the evil we have done; condemn us not for all the good we have omitted; but, for the sake of Thy beloved Son, in whom we have redemption through His blood, receive us graciously, and love us freely.

Almighty God, who workest in us to will and to do of Thy good pleasure, give us grace that we may truly repent of all our sins, and heartily yield ourselves up to Thy service. Let it be the work of our whole lives to obey Thee—the joy of our souls to please Thee—the satisfaction of all our desires, and the fulfilment of all our hopes, to walk with Thee in the comforts of Thy fellowship, and to dwell with Thee in the glories of Thy kingdom.

O God, who art light, and in whom is no darkness at all, shine into our hearts, we beseech Thee, by Thy Holy Spirit, and cause us, in Thy light, clearly to see light. Deliver us from ignorance, error, and unbelief; dispose us, as children of light and of the day, to renounce the hidden things of dishonesty, and to have no fellowship with the unfruitful works of darkness; enable us to walk in truth and uprightness, in purity and sincerity, before Thee, that our fellowship may be with Thee, the Father, and with Thy Son, Jesus Christ; and that, when the shadows of this life have passed away, we may enjoy the vision of Thy heavenly glory, and may ourselves shine forth, with the brightness of the sun, in Thy kingdom for ever and ever.

Almighty God, who hast spared us in Thy providence to see another return of Thy holy day, make us thankful for this precious season of hallowed rest and spiritual improvement; and enable us by Thy grace to sanctify it, to the honour of Thy name and the good of our own souls. Cause us to rejoice, when it is said unto us, Go ye up into the house of the Lord; and teach us to esteem a day spent in Thy courts as better than a thousand elsewhere. Give grace to Thy ministering servants rightly to divide Thy Word of truth; and let their preaching be accompanied with the power and demonstration of Thy Holy Spirit.

Draw nigh to those who are necessarily withheld from worshipping Thee in the congregation of Thy people, and make them glad with the light of Thy countenance. Have pity on those who neglect or forsake Thine ordinances; cause them yet to seek Thee whilst Thou art to be found, and to call upon Thee whilst Thou art near. Look with compassion on the whole of our fallen race. Send forth the light of Thy Gospel into every land, and pour out the grace of Thy Spirit upon all flesh, that Thy righteousness may be openly shown in the sight of the heathen, and that the whole earth may be filled with Thy glory.

These, our humble supplications, we present to Thee, in the name of Jesus, Thy beloved Son, to whom, with Thee and with the Holy Spirit, be honour and praise, dominion and blessing, for ever and ever.—Amen.

Lord's Day Evening.

ALMIGHTY GOD, who hast this day permitted us to enjoy the hallowed rest of Thy Sabbath, and to partake of the blessedness of the man whom Thou causest to approach unto Thee, that he may dwell in Thy courts; we give Thee thanks for the privileges Thou hast conferred, and humbly implore the grace of Thy Holy Spirit, that we may be enabled to profit by the use of them.

We bless Thee that we have a great High Priest, who beareth the iniquity of our holy things; and we beseech Thee to pardon for His sake the manifold sins and imperfections of our sacred duties. Graciously receive the tribute of our worship, notwithstanding all the wanderings of thought and coldness of affection with which it has been rendered. And grant that the saving truths of Thy Word, though often heard with listlessness and inattention, may be fixed in our memories and impressed upon our hearts, and that, as precious seed sown in a good soil, they may bring forth fruit abundantly to Thy praise.

O our God, we have cause to be ashamed that hitherto we have profited so little by the lessons of Thy Word and the worship of Thy house. Let them not rise against us to our condemnation; but grant that our growth in knowledge and in grace may henceforth be in some measure answerable to the opportunities and advantages Thou hast afforded us, and that by our continual advancement in godliness we may be enabled to show forth the praises of Him who hath called us out of darkness into His marvellous light.

Almighty Saviour, in whom all fulness dwells, we humbly beseech Thee that it may be given us to receive out of Thy fulness grace sufficient for us; so that, being taught of Thee how we ought to walk and to please God, we may abound therein more and more. Cause us to be filled with the knowledge of Thy will in all wisdom and spiritual understanding. Strengthen our faith; enliven our hope; increase our love; perfect our repentance. Suffer us not to rest satisfied with present attainments; but carry us still forward in Thy ways, until we are fit to be translated to that better country where we shall see Thee face to face, and, being fully conformed to Thine image, shall love Thee supremely, rejoice in Thee triumphantly, and celebrate Thy praises for ever.

We pray for all our brethren of mankind, that they may be brought to the knowledge of Thy truth. Be merciful to the land in which we dwell. Multiply Thy blessings on our Sovereign and her family. Be gracious to all who minister in holy things, that they may watch for souls as those who must give account. Visit in mercy the children of affliction; supply their wants; relieve their sufferings; give unto them patience and submission to Thy blessed will; and in Thy good time deliver them from all their troubles.

Take us, we beseech Thee, and all who are dear to us, into Thy fatherly protection this night. Defend us from danger; grant us quiet sleep; and, if it please Thee, spare us to enjoy the blessings and to discharge the duties of another day.

Graciously hear us, O God, and have mercy on us, for the sake of Thy beloved Son, our strength, and our Redeemer.—Amen.

Monday Morning.

ALMIGHTY GOD, our heavenly Father, who hast safely brought us to the beginning of this day; continue to us, throughout the course of it, Thy fatherly guidance and protection. Defend us from all danger; keep us from all sin; and so direct and govern us by Thy Holy Spirit, that we may walk in uprightness before Thee, and do always that which is pleasing in Thy sight.

We confess, O God, that we are prone to forget Thee amidst the concerns and business of our daily life, and that we have in many things grievously offended Thee by our wilful disobedience to Thy commandments. Pardon, we beseech Thee, for the sake of Thy beloved Son, our manifold sins and shortcomings in the time that is past; and enable us henceforth more constantly to remember Thee, and with greater diligence and faithfulness to serve Thee.

Help us to enter on the labours of the week in the spirit of those devout exercises in which we were yesterday occupied in Thy house, and of those holy lessons which were addressed to us from Thy Word. Teach us to acknowledge Thee in all our ways, that Thou mayest direct our paths. Whether we be called to rule or to obey, to teach or to learn, to labour or to suffer, enable us in our several callings to abide with Thee. And whatsoever we do, dispose us to do it heartily, as to the Lord, and not unto men.

Father of mercies, receive our humble thanks for all the benefits, temporal and spiritual, which from day to day Thou art graciously bestowing on us; and enable us to show our gratitude, not only by the praises of our lips, but by the cheerful obedience of our hearts and lives.

[To Thy fatherly care we commend the children of this family. Preserve them from the dangers and temptations to which, in an evil world, they are exposed. Cause them to grow in grace, and in the knowledge of Jesus Christ, whom to know is life eternal.

We implore Thy blessing on the servants of this household, beseeching Thee to aid and encourage them in all their duties, and to make them faithful followers of Him who took upon Him the form of a servant, and went about doing good.]

Graciously hear our intercessions, O God, for all conditions and orders of our fellow-men; for the Queen and all in authority over us, that they may rule as Thy ministers to us for good; for the pastors of Thy flock, that they may be faithful and successful; for our friends and kindred, that it may please Thee to remember them for good, and to visit them with Thy salvation; for those who are in adversity and affliction, that they may be blessed with the comforts of Thy Word and Spirit; and for all men, that they may be brought to the knowledge, faith, and obedience of Thy Gospel.

These our humble supplications we present to Thee, O Thou that hearest prayer. Graciously answer them for the sake of Jesus Christ, our Lord and Saviour.—Amen.

Monday Evening.

ALMIGHTY GOD, who art the confidence of all the ends of the earth, and of them that are afar off upon the sea—our Sun and Shield, our refuge and defence, the strength of our heart, and the Rock of our Salvation—enable us to put our trust in Thee. Teach us with full assurance to look up to Thee as our reconciled God and Father in Christ Jesus, who art willing, for His sake, to supply our utmost need. And graciously remember Thy Word unto Thy servants, on which Thou hast caused us to hope, that Thou wilt keep him in perfect peace whose mind is stayed upon Thee.

We confess, O God, that hitherto we have been prone to trust in the creature more than in the Creator. We have leant for support and succour on an arm of flesh. We have looked for guidance to the counsels of earthly wisdom. And instead of humbly acknowledging our dependence on Thee, we have often placed an unwarranted reliance on the might of our own efforts and the sufficiency of our own resources.

Pardon, O God, for the sake of Thy beloved Son, whatever want of confidence we have shown towards Thee; and lead us henceforth by the teaching of Thy Holy Spirit to trust in Thee with all our hearts. Help us to rely on the goodness of Thy providence. Increase our faith in the promises of Thy Word. Dispose us cheerfully to cast upon Thee all our cares, humbly to commit to Thy keeping all our interests, and earnestly to seek the aid of Thy strength and the guidance of Thy wisdom in all our undertakings. Above all, teach us wholly to depend on the merciful provisions of Thy

Gospel for the everlasting welfare of our souls. Counting all things but loss for the excellency of the knowledge of Christ Jesus our Lord, may we seek to win Christ, and to be found in Him, not having our own righteousness which is of the law, but that which is through the faith of Christ, even the righteousness which is of God by faith. Convince us that without Him we can do nothing, but that through His strength we can do all things. And cause us to know Him whom we have believed, so as to be persuaded that he is able to keep unto the great day that which we have committed to Him; and that neither death, nor life, nor angels, nor principalities, nor powers, nor things present, nor things to come, nor height, nor depth, nor any other creature, shall be able to separate us from the love of God, which is in Christ Jesus our Lord.

And now, O God, we commend ourselves to Thy care. We will lay ourselves down in peace, and sleep, because Thou only makest us to dwell in safety. Take us, and all who are near and dear to us, now and evermore, under Thy protection. Extend Thy special help and pity to those who are in circumstances of distress. Reveal Thy marvellous light to such as are in darkness. Increase everywhere the number of Thy faithful people; and let all those that trust in Thee rejoice, because with favour Thou wilt compass them as with a shield.

Graciously hear the voice of our supplications, which we offer in the name of Thy well-beloved Son, our Lord and Saviour.—Amen.

Tuesday Morning.

O GOD, who hast taught us to be careful for nothing, but in everything, by prayer and supplication with thanksgiving, to make our requests known unto Thee; we cast ourselves this morning on Thy care, and humbly ask of Thee those things which are necessary as well for the body as the soul.

Holy Father, we are not worthy to come into Thy sacred presence by reason of our manifold offences, much less to receive any favour at Thy hands. But we put our trust in the merits of Thy beloved Son, who gave Himself as a sacrifice for our sins; and for His sake we earnestly beseech Thee to take away all our iniquity and receive us graciously, and to supply all our need according to Thy glorious riches by Christ Jesus.

O God, who knowest that while we are in this life we have manifold bodily wants to be supplied, and hast graciously promised to them that seek first Thy kingdom and the righteousness thereof, that all other needful things shall be added to them; grant us such a competent portion of earthly blessings as Thy wisdom seeth to be suitable and expedient for us. We ask of Thee neither poverty nor riches, but food to eat and raiment to put on. Give to us skill and industry to provide for ourselves and for those of our own house who are dependent on us. Bless us in all the works of our hands, that we may have sufficient not to be chargeable, but rather to be helpful to others. And whatsoever in Thy providence Thou sendest, make us to be heartily content with Thy blessed will. Suffer us not in prosperity to forget Thee, or in adversity to think ourselves forgotten of Thee. Teach us to acknowledge and adore Thee in all Thy gifts; and when earthly comforts fail, to joy evermore in the God of our salvation. Above all, grant that our spiritual wants may be more and more abundantly supplied through the fulness of the blessings of Thy Gospel, to the end that, growing in knowledge and in grace, our souls may be strengthened and nourished unto life eternal.

We pray not only for ourselves, but for our brethren, that it may please Thee to succour and relieve them according to their several necessities. Give food to the hungry, clothing to the naked, instruction to the ignorant, comfort to the sorrowful, health to the sick, and hope to the dying.

[Bestow Thy blessing on the labours of the husbandman; and grant unto us favourable weather and fruitful seasons, that our fields may in due time yield an abundant increase.]

Bless our native land with plenty and prosperity. Enrich with Thy favour our Sovereign the Queen. Give to all ranks and conditions of the people such temporal and spiritual blessings as are needful for them. Regard in Thy mercy the whole human race; and bring them to the knowledge and obedience of Thy truth.

Hear us, O God, and grant an answer of peace, for the sake of Thy beloved Son, our Lord and Saviour.—Amen.

Tuesday Evening.

ALMIGHTY GOD, who orderest all things in heaven and on earth according to Thy wise counsel, give us grace that we may reverently adore and cheerfully submit to Thy most blessed will. Teach us to acknowledge that Thou art just in all Thy ways, and holy in all Thy works; and although clouds and darkness are about Thee, give us to rejoice that righteousness and judgment are the habitation of Thy throne, and that mercy and truth go before Thy face.

We confess, O God, that we have been slow of heart to recognise the wisdom and goodness of Thy dealings with us; that we have often been discontented with our own condition, and have looked with envy and uncharitableness on the good of others; and that, instead of meekly bowing to Thy will, we have, by our repining dispositions and covetous affections, oftentimes rebelled against Thee.

Pardon, O God, wherein we have thus offended Thee. Graciously receive us through the merits of Thy beloved Son, in whom we have redemption through His blood. Blot out for His sake our manifold provocations, and remember our iniquities no more.

Give us grace also, whereby we may be enabled wholly to give ourselves up to Thy disposal. Make us willing that Thou shouldst choose our portion for us. Confirm our faith in the assurance Thou hast given us, that all Thy ways are mercy and truth to such as keep Thy covenant and Thy testimonies, and that all things work together for good to them that love Thee. Grant us deliverance from anxious cares, and envious tempers, and inordinate affections. And teach us in whatsoever state we are, therewith to be content; that everywhere, and in all things, we may be instructed both to be full and to be hungry, both to abound and to suffer need.

O God, who hast prepared for us in heaven a better and more enduring substance than can be found on earth; dispose us to seek those things which are above, where Christ sitteth at Thy right hand; and enable us so to look, not at the things which are seen and temporal, but at the things which are unseen and eternal, that we may bear patiently all present hardships, and may reckon them unworthy to be compared with the glory which shall hereafter be revealed in us.

Father of mercies, we thankfully acknowledge Thy goodness to us throughout the past day; and during this night we humbly commit ourselves, and all whom we love, to Thy fatherly protection. Suffer no evil to befall us, nor any plague to come nigh our dwelling.

We pray for the several members of this household, that they may prosper in all things and be in health; above all, that their souls may prosper.

We pray for the sick, the sorrowful, and the dying, that it may please Thee to comfort and support them.

We pray for the whole family of mankind, that Thou wouldst mercifully enlighten and convert them, and bless them in Christ Jesus with spiritual and heavenly blessings.

Incline Thine ear, O God, to our supplications, which we offer in the name of Thy beloved Son, our Lord and only Saviour.—Amen.

Wednesday Morning.

O THOU that hearest prayer, unto Thee shall all flesh come. We thank Thee that we have a great High Priest, who ever liveth to make intercession for us. And in His name we earnestly beseech Thee to pardon our sins, to help our infirmities, and to bestow upon us whatsoever things Thou knowest in Thy wisdom to be needful or expedient for us.

Blessed be Thou, O God and Father of our Lord Jesus Christ, who hast blessed us in Him with all spiritual blessings. Grant that we may in everything be enriched by Him, so as to be complete in Christ. And to this end convince us of our need of Him; show us His divine fulness and His sufficiency for our spiritual wants; cause us to be persuaded in our hearts that there is no salvation in any other; and dispose us to receive and rest on Him alone, as able and willing to save us unto the uttermost.

Lord, we believe; help Thou our unbelief. Pardon the weakness and unsteadfastness of our faith. Make it more firm, and lively, and effectual; that we may be filled with all joy and peace in believing, and may be fruitful in every good work.

God of all grace, enable us this day, and all the days of our sojourning in the body, to live by faith in the Son of God, who loved us, and gave Himself for us. Give us grace continually to abide in Him, that we may bear much fruit. And whatsoever we do, in word or deed dispose us to do all in the name of the Lord Jesus, giving thanks to God, even the Father, by Him.

Graciously hear our intercessions, we beseech Thee,

for those whom we ought to remember at Thy throne of grace. Bestow thy favour on all our beloved friends. Impart relief and comfort to the afflicted. Instruct the ignorant; reclaim the erring; build up Thy saints in their most holy faith.

[Bestow Thy blessing on the children of this family. Keep them from the snares and dangers of an evil world; and cause them to grow in knowledge and in grace.

Regard with Thy favour the servants of this household, and enable them, in their appointed stations, faithfully to serve and honour Thee, their Master in heaven.]

Bless our Queen, and all in authority over us. Extend Thy favour and protection to our country. Bless Thy whole Church throughout the world. Watch over Thy flock wherever they be scattered; gather in both Jews and Gentiles into Thy fold; and hasten the time when there shall be one fold and one Shepherd.

These, our humble supplications, we present to Thee, in the name and through the mediation of Jesus Christ our Lord and Saviour.—Amen.

Wednesday Evening.

WHOM have we, O God, in heaven but Thee? and there is none upon earth that we desire besides Thee. Our flesh and our heart faileth; but Thou art the strength of our heart, and our portion for ever.

We worship Thee as the greatest and best of Beings, the perfection of all excellence, and the source of all goodness. And we beseech Thee to manifest Thyself to us, in the adorable attributes of Thy character, and in the exceeding abundance of Thy tender mercies, so that we may be led more heartily to love Thee, and more worthily to magnify Thy blessed name.

We acknowledge, O God, that our hearts have been estranged from Thee; that we have been regardless of Thy claims, indifferent to Thine excellences, and unthankful for Thy benefits; that we have allowed the vanities of the world to rob Thee of our homage and affection; that we have preferred the indulgence of our sinful desires to the enjoyment of Thy favour and loving-kindness, which are better than life.

Merciful Father, who hast given Thine own Son to be the propitiation for sins, grant us for His sake Thy mercy to forgive us, and Thy grace to help us according to our need. Pardon all the defects of our love to Thee, and all the excesses of our love to earthly things. Turn our inclinations and affections from those vain objects which would draw away our hearts from Thee. Give to us clear views of Thine excellency; impress us with a lively sense of Thy goodness. Above all, teach us to comprehend, with all saints, the breadth, and length, and depth, and height of Thine immeasurable love in our redemption.

And cause us to love Thee, who hast so loved us, with all our heart, and with all our soul, and with all our mind, and with all our strength, and to show our love by keeping Thy commandments.

God of all grace, without whom we can do nothing, enable us to continue in Thy love; and cause our love to abound yet more and more in knowledge and in all judgment; that we may approve things that are excellent; that we may prefer Thy favour above our chief joy; that we may delight to do Thy blessed will; that we may be filled with the fruits of righteousness, which are by Jesus Christ unto the praise and glory of our God.

Father of mercies, we give Thee special thanks for what of Thy love Thou hast this day conferred upon us. And we beseech Thee, during this night, to take us and all who are dear to us under Thy protection.

O God, who art very pitiful and of tender mercy, look with compassion on all who are afflicted. Heal the sick; provide for the destitute; deliver the oppressed; prepare the dying for their change.

Let Thy way, O God, be known upon the earth, and Thy saving health among all nations. Gather in the dispersed of Israel, with the fulness of the Gentiles, into Thy fold. And add to Thy Church daily such as shall be saved.

Mercifully hear us, O God, and accept of us, for the Lord Jesus' sake.—Amen.

Thursday Morning.

O LORD our God, whose name is Holy, and in whose presence evil cannot dwell; we bow ourselves before Thee this morning under a deep sense of our sinfulness, and humbly implore of Thee mercy to pardon, and grace to help us according to our need.

O our God, we are ashamed to lift up our faces unto Thee; for our consciences accuse us, and our sins witness against us. We confess that our hearts are corrupt and depraved, and that there is no soundness in us. We acknowledge that there is a law in our members, warring against the law of our mind, and bringing us into captivity to the law of sin. We deeply lament that when we would do good evil is present with us; and that through the power of the sins that do beset us, we are often and easily turned from Thy ways, and led to do that which is hateful in Thy sight.

Father of mercies, we beseech Thee to have compassion on us. Be pleased, for the sake of Jesus Christ, Thy well-beloved Son, to blot out all our sins; and to bestow upon us the grace of Thy Holy Spirit, whereby we may be wholly renewed after Thine image, and may be enabled more and more to die unto sin and live unto righteousness. Grant that our old man may be crucified with Christ, that the body of sin may be destroyed. And like as Christ was raised up from the dead, so may we also walk in newness of life. Suffer not sin any longer to reign in our mortal bodies, that we should obey it in the lusts thereof. Enable us to crucify the flesh, with all its evil desires and affections. And grant that, being made free from sin, and having become servants to God, we may have our fruit unto holiness, and the end everlasting life.

Almighty God, who givest power to the faint, and increasest strength to them that have no might, we look to Thee for countenance and aid in whatsoever duties or trials may await us. Fulfil to us now and always Thy promise, that, as our day, so shall our strength be. Arm us with might to resist every temptation, and to lay aside every besetting sin. And stablish our hearts in every good word and work, that we may stand perfect and complete in all Thy will.

Bestow Thy favour, we beseech Thee, on our friends and kindred, [especially on the children of this family.] Bless them, and keep them, and make Thy face to shine upon them. Extend Thy pity to the sick and the afflicted. Comfort the mourners. Support and prepare the dying.

O God, who wouldst have all men to come to the knowledge of the truth, let Thy Word everywhere have free course and be glorified; and hasten the time when all the kingdoms of this world shall become the kingdoms of our Lord and of His Christ.

Graciously hear us, O God, and accept of us, through Jesus Christ, our only Mediator, to whom, with Thee and with the Holy Spirit, be glory everlasting.—Amen.

Thursday Evening.

O THOU that dwellest in the heavens, unto Thee we lift up our souls. We thank Thee for the encouragement Thou hast given us to come with boldness unto the throne of grace; and for the assurance that if men, being evil, know how to give good gifts unto their children, much more will our heavenly Father give the Holy Spirit to them that ask Him.

Grant us, we pray Thee, this great gift, which we ask in the name of Thy well-beloved Son. Let Thy Spirit be shed on us abundantly through Jesus Christ our Saviour. Let Him be unto us a Spirit of light and truth, to guide us to the clear understanding of Thy mind and will; a Spirit of power to quicken and convert us, and to strengthen us with all needful might in the inner man; a Spirit of comfort to cheer us in our times of trouble; a Spirit of holiness to purify us more and more, and to make us fruitful in every good work.

Pardon, O God, wherein we have offended Thee by grieving or resisting Thy Spirit. Suffer us not to do despite unto Him, lest He should cease to strive with us any more. Cast us not away from Thy presence, and take not Thy Holy Spirit from us. But grant that He may abide with us continually, making us to grow in knowledge and in grace, and filling us with His blessed and holy fruits, which are in all goodness and righteousness and truth.

O Thou God of all grace, who hast called us unto the adoption of children by Jesus Christ, and hast given us in Him exceeding great and precious promises, we earnestly pray that Thy Holy Spirit may witness with our spirits that we are Thy children. And we beseech Thee to seal us with that Spirit of promise, which is the earnest of our inheritance, until the redemption of the purchased possession, unto the praise of Thy glory.

Hear our intercessions, O God, in behalf of all our brethren of mankind. Pour out Thy Holy Spirit upon all flesh, that the wilderness may become a fruitful field, and that the whole earth may be filled with Thy glory, Pour out Thy Holy Spirit upon all the Churches, that Thy work may be more and more revived in them. Impart the consolations of Thy Spirit to all whom Thou hast visited with affliction, that they may be strengthened, according to His glorious power, unto all patience and long-suffering with joyfulness. Give unto all Thy people, we beseech Thee, the grace of Thy Holy Spirit in such measures as Thy divine wisdom seeth to be needful for building them up in their most holy faith, and for enabling them steadfastly to abide with Thee in the stations which Thy providence hath allotted to them.

And now, O God, we humbly commit ourselves, and all whom we love, to Thy fatherly care. Grant us refreshing sleep; shield us from all evil; and bring us in peace to the light of a new day.

Graciously hear us, O God, and have mercy upon us, for the Lord Jesus' sake.—Amen.

Friday Morning.

ALMIGHTY GOD, who dwellest in the light to which no man can approach; in whose presence there is no night, in the light of whose countenance there is perpetual day; we, Thy servants, whom Thou hast preserved during the past night, and who live by Thy power, desire this morning to bless Thee for the defence of Thy watchful providence; and humbly pray Thee to grant that this day, and all the days of our life, may be holy and peaceable, healthful to our bodies and profitable to our souls.

O Lord our God, we are sinful creatures, unworthy of Thy favour; but we are sorrowful and repenting. And though Thou hast just cause to be angry with us, yet in Christ Jesus hath Thine anger been turned away. Be pleased, O God, for the sake of Thy beloved Son, to blot out all our sins from Thy remembrance, and to heal our souls that we may sin against Thee no more. Open our eyes that we may see our infirmities; make us watchful against them; enable us to amend them; and give us perfect understanding in the way of godliness, that we may walk in it all the days of our pilgrimage. Dispose us to be faithful and diligent in our several callings; cheerful and zealous in duty; patient in trial; charitable in temper; pure and sincere in speech; fervent in prayer, and ready to every good work. And whether we eat or drink, or whatsoever we do, enable us to do all to Thy glory.

Let Thy good providence continually watch over us, that we may be delivered from all evil. Enable us so to spend this day, that it may be profitable both to ourselves and others, and may leave with us no sorrow or evil conscience at its close. And grant that we may, throughout our whole life, be so directed and governed by Thy Holy Spirit, that when the time of our short abode on earth is ended, we may die in Thy favour, and rest in a holy hope, and finally obtain the joys of a blessed resurrection.

Regard with Thy favour our family, our neighbourhood, our country, our Queen, and all in authority over us. Bless Thy Church Universal. Unite the hearts of all Thy faithful people as the heart of one man in the belief and love of Thy truth. And hasten the prevalence of Thy kingdom among all nations.

God of all comfort, have pity on the afflicted; assuage their griefs; relieve their sufferings; and overrule Thy chastening for their good.

Graciously hear and answer us, O Lord, according to the fulness of Thy mercy in Christ Jesus, our Lord and Saviour.—Amen.

Friday Evening.

ETERNAL GOD, Father of men and angels, by whose care and providence we are preserved and blessed, comforted and assisted; we heartily thank Thee for the many temporal and spiritual mercies Thou hast bestowed upon us this day. Suffer us not to be forgetful of Thy benefits; and though we are not worthy of the least of them, be pleased still to remember us for good.

Pardon, we beseech Thee, for the sake of Thy beloved Son, the sins and follies we have this day committed against Thee; the unprofitableness of our services, the strength of our passions, the uncharitableness of our tempers, the rashness of our words, the vanity and evil of our actions. Alas! O God, how long shall we confess our sins, and pray against them, while yet we fall under them? O suffer it to be so no more. Let us never return to those iniquities of which we are ashamed, and which bring sorrow and death. Give us a command over our evil inclinations, a perfect hatred of sin, and a love to Thee above all the desires of this world. Let it be the great employment of our lives to honour and serve Thee. And let our rejoicing be the testimony of our conscience, that in simplicity and godly sincerity, not with fleshly wisdom, but by the grace of God, we have our conversation in the world.

O Thou keeper of Israel, who never slumberest, watch over us, and over all who are near and dear to us, this night. Shield us from all harm; keep us from all sin; and whether we sleep or wake, let us live with Thee. Fulfil Thy promise, that Thou wilt never leave us nor forsake us. Enable us to pass the time of our sojourning in Thy faith, fear, and love; and when we die, receive us into Thy hands, O holy and ever-blessed Jesus, that we may dwell in Thy presence, and behold Thy face, and sing praises unto Thy name for ever.

[We implore Thy blessing on the children of this family. Teach them to remember Thee in the days of youth; and keep them by Thy power through faith unto salvation.

Enable the servants of this household, we beseech Thee, to show all good fidelity in their appointed stations. And whatsoever they do, dispose them to do it heartily, as unto the Lord, and not unto man.]

Father of mercies and God of all comfort, look with compassion on the sick and the afflicted. Give them support and comfort in their trials; and overrule Thy fatherly chastening to the everlasting welfare of their souls.

Bless our Queen, our rulers, and our country. Pardon our many national sins; continue to regard us with Thy favour; and make us a people fearing Thee and working righteousness.

Bless Thy whole Church. Unite all Christians in the bonds of a common faith and love. And speedily fill the whole earth with Thy glory.

Give ear, O God, to our humble supplications, for the sake of our only Mediator, Jesus Christ; to whom, with Thee and with the Holy Spirit, be honour and glory for evermore.—Amen.

Saturday Morning.

ALMIGHTY GOD, our heavenly Father, who hast watched over us during the past night, and hast spared us in the enjoyment of many blessings to another day; we render praise and thanks to Thee for all Thy goodness. We acknowledge Thee as the Father of lights, from whom cometh down every good and every perfect gift; who forgivest our iniquities, who healest our diseases, who redeemest our life from destruction, who satisfiest our mouth with good things, who crownest us with loving-kindness and tender mercies.

Pardon, O God, for the sake of Thy beloved Son, our past ingratitude for Thy benefits. Impress us henceforth with a more lively sense of them, that our souls may be stirred up to bless Thy holy name. Fill us with love to Thee, who hast first loved us. And teach us, as becometh the children of so many mercies, to be kind and compassionate towards our fellow-men, loving them out of a pure and fervent heart, and doing them good as we have opportunity.

Above all, give us a deep and abiding sense of the love of Christ, which passeth knowledge; and grant that it may constrain us by Thy grace to walk in love, as Christ also loved us. Dispose us to bear one another's burdens, so as to fulfil the law of Christ. Help us to remember the words of the Lord Jesus, that it is more blessed to give than to receive; and make us willing, if need be, to deny ourselves, so as the more abundantly to supply the wants of others. Teach us, as much as lieth in us, to live peaceably with all men, recompensing to no man evil for evil, but overcoming evil with good. Let all bitterness, and wrath, and anger, and clamour, and evil-speaking be put away from us, with all malice; and make us kind, tender-hearted, and forgiving, even as Thou for Christ's sake forgivest us.

[We implore Thy blessing on all the members of this family, that they may be kindly affected one towards another, and may find how good and pleasant a thing it is to dwell together as brethren in unity.]

We pray for the welfare and happiness of our Sovereign; for the peace and prosperity of our country; for the speedy enlightenment and conversion of all nations.

We beseech Thee to look with compassion on the afflicted, and to grant them all needful relief and consolation.

[Father of mercies, who openest Thy hand and satisfiest the desire of every living thing, command Thy blessing on the labours of the husbandman; and grant unto us seasonable weather, that the fruits of the earth may be fully matured and safely gathered.]

And now, O God, we commit ourselves to Thee. Watch over us this day; deliver us from all danger; aid us in our lawful occupations; and keep our souls unspotted from the world.

Grant these requests, O Father, we beseech Thee, which we humbly present in the name of Thy beloved Son, our Lord and Saviour.—Amen.

Saturday Evening.

ALMIGHTY GOD, by whose good hand upon us we have hitherto been guided in our pilgrimage, we give Thee praise and thanks for all the blessings which during the week now drawing to a close, and throughout the whole of our past life, Thou hast conferred upon us. We acknowledge that we are not worthy of the least of all Thy benefits. But so much the more do we magnify Thy name for having dealt so bountifully with us.

Pardon, O God, for the sake of Thy beloved Son, our oft-repeated trespasses and sins, whereby we have provoked Thee to withdraw Thy mercies from us; and give us grace, that henceforth we may be enabled to bring forth fruits meet for repentance, and to show our gratitude for Thine unceasing goodness by a cheerful and constant obedience to Thy holy will.

Blessed Lord, who art of power to stablish us according to Thy Gospel, strengthen our hearts that we fall not from our steadfastness. Hold Thou us up, and so we shall be safe. Suffer us no more to wander from Thy ways, or to grow weary in keeping Thy commandments. Whatever of sin or of infirmity Thou seest in us, O Lord, forgive it, and help us to overcome it. Whatever of good Thy grace may have wrought in us, be pleased to confirm and complete it unto the day of Christ. Make us watchful against temptation; strong in faith; diligent in duty; patient in trial; and fervent in prayer. Teach us to endure hardness as good soldiers of Jesus Christ; and to take unto us the whole armour of God, that we may be able to withstand in the evil day, and having done all to stand.

O Thou that savest by Thy right hand them that put their trust in Thee from those that rise up against them, grant us defence and deliverance, we beseech Thee, from all the enemies that war against the soul. Let thy divine power so strengthen our weakness, that neither the craft of the devil, nor the allurements of the world, nor the evil desires of our own hearts, may prevail against us, but that we may in all things be more than conquerors through Him that loved us. Keep us steadfast and immovable, always abounding in the work of the Lord; and enable us to be faithful unto death, that we may receive the crown of life.

Hear our intercessions, we beseech Thee, in behalf of all our brethren of mankind. We pray for the nations that are sitting in gross darkness, that it may please Thee to bring them into Thy marvellous light. We pray for Thy Church Universal, and more especially for the Church of our fathers, that truth and godliness may flourish in it more and more, and that its members, united in the bonds of love, may dwell together as brethren in unity. We pray for those whom Thou hast visited with affliction, that it may please Thee to comfort and relieve them, and to overrule the trials they are now enduring for the everlasting health and welfare of their souls. We pray for the several members of this family, and for all who by the ties of kindred are connected with them, that they may be blessed with the joys of Thy favour, and sanctified by the grace of Thy Holy Spirit, and kept by Thy power through faith unto salvation.

And now, O God, we beseech Thee to watch over us, and over all who are dear to us, this night. Preserve us from all evil; grant us refreshing sleep; and if it please Thee, spare us to enjoy the blessings, and fit us to discharge the duties, of Thy holy day.

These, our humble supplications, we present in the name and through the mediation of Jesus Christ, our Lord and Saviour —Amen.

THIRD WEEK.

Lord's Day Morning.

ALMIGHTY GOD, who hast spared us to see another return of the Christian Sabbath; we give Thee thanks for the privileges which on this sacred day Thou art pleased to bestow upon us, and humbly implore the grace of Thy Holy Spirit, that we may worthily use them, for our good and for Thy glory.

This is the day which the Lord hath made; we will rejoice and be glad in it. Save now, we beseech Thee, O Lord; O Lord, we beseech Thee, send now prosperity. Glory be to Thee, O God, who didst, as on this day, raise up Thy Son from the dead, and give Him glory, that our faith and hope might be in Thee. Thou art our God, and we will praise Thee; Thou art our God, we will exalt Thee. O give thanks unto the Lord; for He is good; for His mercy endureth for ever.

Holy, holy, holy, Lord God of Hosts; the whole earth is full of Thy glory. Thou hast prepared Thy throne in the heavens, and Thy kingdom ruleth over all. Honour and majesty are before Thee; strength and beauty are in Thy sanctuary. Help us to give the glory that is due to Thee, who art the former of our bodies and the Father of our spirits, the giver of every good and perfect gift, the strength of our life, and the Rock of our Salvation.

O our God, we are ashamed, and blush to lift up our faces unto Thee. Our hearts condemn us, and our sins witness against us. Behold! we are men of unclean lips, and we dwell in the midst of a people of unclean lips; and we are not worthy to approach Thy presence, or to utter Thy blessed name. Neither are we able of ourselves to render any acceptable service to Thee. When we would do good, evil is present with us. Our souls cleave to the dust, when we would lift them up to heaven. Innumerable worldly thoughts intrude upon us, even in our most devout exercises. And often, when the words of prayer are on our lips, our hearts are far from Thee.

O Lord, with whom is forgiveness that Thou mayest be feared, and plenteous redemption; have mercy upon us.

O God, who hast not appointed us to wrath, but to obtain salvation by our Lord Jesus Christ; have mercy upon us.

Remember not against us former transgressions; but according to Thy mercy remember Thou us, for Thy goodness' sake, O Lord. Justify us freely by Thy grace through the redemption that is in Christ Jesus. And grant that, through the intercession of Thy beloved Son, and by the effectual working of Thy Holy Spirit, our prayers and praises may be well pleasing in Thy sight.

Father of mercies, receive our humble and hearty thanks for all Thy goodness. We bless Thy name, that Thou hast bountifully provided for us, not only such things as are serviceable for the body, but such also as are needful for the soul. We thank Thee for the holy rest of Thy Day, for the instructions of Thy Word, for the ordinances of Thy worship, for the promised grace of Thy Holy Spirit, and above all, for Jesus Christ, Thine unspeakable gift, in whom Thou hast blessed us with all spiritual and heavenly blessings. Forbid, O God, that the privileges we enjoy should rise up against us to our condemnation. Grant that our profiting by them may appear in a life of consistent obedience to Thy will; and that all the institutions and observances of Thy Church on earth may prepare us for the higher and purer worship of the Church in heaven.

O Lord, who hast said that where two or three are gathered together in Thy name, there art Thou in the midst of them, be present this day in all the assemblies of Thy people. Let Thy Word everywhere have free course and be glorified. Assist Thy ministering servants in proclaiming it; and open the hearts of all Thy people, for the humble, faithful, and profitable reception of it.

Draw nigh to such as are necessarily withheld from joining in the public worship of Thy Church; and grant unto them, in the retirement of their dwellings, the joy of Thy favour and the comfort of Thy fellowship. Have pity on those who wilfully forsake or profane Thine ordinances, and bring them to repentance. Increase everywhere the number of Thy true worshippers; and hasten the time when, throughout the whole world, Thy name shall be honoured, and Thy Word believed and obeyed.

Incline Thine ear, O God, to our supplications, which we offer in the name of Thy beloved Son, our Lord and Saviour.—Amen.

Lord's Day Evening.

ALMIGHTY GOD, who hast given us all things that pertain unto life and godliness, we thank Thee for the hallowed rest of another Sabbath, and for our renewed opportunities this day of hearing Thy Word, and showing forth Thy praise.

Pardon, we beseech Thee, whatever Thy pure eye hath seen to be amiss in our attempts to serve Thee. Enter not into judgment with us, O Lord, for the weakness of our faith, the wandering of our thoughts, the levity of our dispositions, the coldness of our affections. But grant, through the merits of our High Priest, who beareth the iniquity of our holy things, that our humble endeavours, though polluted with much sin, and marred by many infirmities and imperfections, may yet, for His sake, be acceptable in Thy sight.

Let it please Thee also to bless for our edification those lessons of divine truth, which have this day been addressed to us. Suffer not the seed of Thy Word to be caught away by the wicked one out of our hearts; but cause it to take such root within us, that it may neither be scorched by the heat of tribulation, nor choked by the cares and pleasures of this life, but that, as precious seed sown in good ground, it may bring forth fruit abundantly to Thy praise.

We confess, O God, that we have often been forgetful and unprofitable hearers of Thy Word; and that we cannot of ourselves receive, as we ought, the things which it declares to us. Pardon, for Christ's sake, the listlessness and inattention wherewith we are prone to regard Thy heavenly teaching. And give us grace, that henceforth we may be enabled to hear Thy Word diligently, to receive it meekly, and to lay it up in our hearts by faith, so as to be made wise unto salvation, and thoroughly furnished unto all good works.

Keep us mindful that Thy Word is designed to be the subject of constant meditation, and the habitual rule of faith and duty. Cause it to dwell in us richly in all wisdom. Imprint its precious truths upon our hearts; and enable us, by the grace of Thy Holy Spirit, to walk more and more in accordance with its precepts.

Graciously hear us, O God, while we plead with Thee, not for ourselves only, but also for our fellow-men. Open, we beseech Thee, a great and effectual door for the preaching of Thy blessed Gospel everywhere. Remove the veil from the hearts of Thine ancient people; dispel the darkness and superstition of the heathen; and hasten the time when all the ends of the earth shall turn to Thee, and all the kindreds of the nations shall worship before Thee. Bless Thy whole Church; heal its divisions; purify it from error and corruption; and grant that the hearts of all its members may be united as the heart of one man, in the belief and love of the truth.

Bestow Thy special blessing, we beseech Thee, on our Sovereign the Queen, the Prince and Princess of Wales, and all the other members of the Royal Family. Give them grace that they may adorn their high station; and make them signal instruments of advancing Thy glory and the public good.

Incline the hearts of Christian parents to bring up their children in the nurture and admonition of the Lord; that they may be prepared rightly to fulfil their several callings in this life, and in the life to come may inherit Thy heavenly kingdom.

[Regard with Thy favour the children of this family. Keep them from the evil that is in the world, and cause them to grow in knowledge and in grace. Enable the servants of this household to honour Thee by a faithful discharge of the duties of their station. And grant that their appointed work may be dignified and sweetened to them, by the thought that in all things they are serving the Lord Christ, from whom they shall receive the reward of the inheritance.]

Give, we beseech Thee, to all Thine afflicted people the supports and consolations of Thy grace. Relieve the sick. Comfort the sorrowful. Supply the wants of the needy. Dispel the fears of the dying, and prepare them for their change.

Be gracious to all of us according to our need. Take us this night under Thy protection. Fulfil to us Thy promise, that Thou wilt never leave nor forsake Thy people. Guide us by Thy counsel while we live, and afterward receive us into glory, through Jesus Christ, in whose name we present our prayers, and to whom, with Thee and with the Holy Spirit, we ascribe all praise and glory, for evermore.—Amen.

Monday Morning.

FATHER of mercies, who hast strengthened and refreshed us by the rest of the past Sabbath and the sleep of the past night, and art now calling us, in the morning of another day, to go forth anew to our ordinary occupations; we render praise to Thee for Thy goodness, and humbly implore the continuance of Thy favour.

Give us grace, that we may walk worthy of Thee unto all pleasing, not only in the observance of Thine ordinances, but in the concerns and business of our daily life. And grant that, throughout the labours of the week, a healthful influence may be exerted on us by the lessons of Thy Word and the solemnities of Thy worship. Suffer us not to esteem any station too humble, or any occupation too common, to furnish opportunities of glorifying Thy name. Keep us mindful that Thou art calling us to serve Thee in whatsoever place Thy providence hath assigned to us. And make us faithful in that which is least, as well as in that which is greatest.

Pardon, O Lord, our proneness to forget Thee amidst the pursuits and engagements of the world. Strengthen us to withstand the temptations that surround us; guard us against the deceitfulness of our own hearts; and enable us, by the grace of Thy Holy Spirit, to acknowledge Thee in all our ways.

Let Thy presence go with us this day to our appointed labours. Make us upright in the discharge of every trust, diligent in the performance of every duty, patient and meek in the endurance of every trial, and steadfast in the resistance of every temptation. Keep us mindful that we are answerable to Thee for the right use of all the faculties, talents, and opportunities of doing good which Thou hast given us. And whatsoever our hand findeth to do, dispose us to do it with our might; not with eye-service as pleasing men, but with singleness of heart as unto Thee.

Be gracious, we beseech Thee, to our relatives and friends. Remember them for good, and visit them with Thy salvation.

Impart relief and comfort to the afflicted. Provide for the poor. Reclaim the erring. Enlighten those who are perishing for lack of knowledge. And speedily diffuse Thy Gospel throughout the world.

Graciously hear us, O God, and have mercy upon us, through Jesus Christ, our Saviour.—Amen.

Monday Evening.

O THOU that hearest prayer, unto Thee shall all flesh come. Bow down Thine ear, O Lord; hear us, for we are poor and needy. Rejoice the souls of Thy servants, for unto Thee do we lift up our souls. For Thou, Lord, art good, and ready to forgive, and plenteous in mercy unto all them that call upon Thee.

O Thou Holy One, with whom evil cannot dwell, we acknowledge and confess before Thee our manifold sins, which in thought, word, and deed, we have oftentimes committed against Thee. All we like sheep have gone astray; we have turned every one to his own way. We have walked in the sight of our own eyes, and have followed the devices and desires of our own hearts. We have slighted Thy counsels, abused Thy mercies, distrusted Thy promises, and broken Thy commandments. And there is not a day of our lives, in which we do not neglect many known duties, and commit many inexcusable offences.

Enter not, O Lord, into judgment with Thy servants, for in Thy sight shall no man living be justified. But let it please Thee, through the merits of Thy beloved Son, who bore our sins in His own body on the tree, to receive us graciously and love us freely.

[Blot out the memory, we beseech Thee, of all the dishonour we have done to Thy law,—of all the despite we have done to Thy grace,—of all the ungrateful returns we have made for Thy goodness,—of all the selfishness, worldliness, and ungodliness, wherewith we have at any time offended Thee. And grant unto us the blessedness of the man whose transgression is forgiven, whose sin is covered, and unto whom Thou imputest not iniquity.]

Gracious God, who desirest not sacrifice, and hast no delight in burnt-offering, but who dost not despise a broken and contrite heart, pour out upon us the grace of Thy Holy Spirit, that we may mourn and be in bitterness because of our trespasses whereby we have trespassed against Thee. And grant that our sorrow may be of that godly sort, which worketh repentance unto salvation not to be repented of. Forbid that we should mock Thee and deceive ourselves, by confessing and lamenting our sins, while we yet cleave to them. Enable us to bring forth fruits meet for repentance. Dispose us to hate and shun every false way, to mortify all sinful inclinations, to resist and subdue all evil habits, and to be ready to every good work. And forasmuch as Thou knowest with how many and how great temptations we are encompassed on every side, and how unable we are to withstand them in our own strength, we pray Thee to uphold us by Thy might, and to make Thy grace sufficient for us, so that we may in all things be more than conquerors, and may in the end obtain the inheritance which Thou hast promised to him that overcometh.

Hear our intercessions, O God, in behalf of all whom Thou hast visited with affliction. Grant them support and comfort in their trials. And let Thy chastening, though for the present grievous, yield in them afterward the peaceable fruits of righteousness.

We more especially commend to Thee all those who are in sorrow and heaviness for their sins. Give them, we beseech Thee, true repentance towards God, and faith unfeigned towards the Lord Jesus Christ. Visit them with the joy of Thy salvation, and uphold them with Thy free Spirit.

We pray for those who are wilfully scorning or thoughtlessly slighting the things which concern their peace, that it may please Thee to awaken and convert them, and to bring them to the knowledge and obedience of Thy Gospel.

Look with compassion, we beseech Thee, on the whole world. Hasten the time when repentance and remission of sins shall be preached in the name of Jesus to all nations, and when men of every tribe shall be blessed in Him and call Him blessed.

O Thou keeper of Israel, who never slumberest, watch over us, and over all who are near and dear to us, this night. Shield us from danger. Grant us quiet sleep. And bring us in safety to the light of another day.

Hear us, O God, and grant an answer of peace, through Jesus Christ, our Saviour.—Amen.

Tuesday Morning.

O GOD, who, though invisible to mortal eye, hast never left Thyself without witness, but hast made Thyself known by the works of Thy hand, the ways of Thy providence, and the revelations of Thy Word; enable us in the name of Jesus to come unto Thee, believing that Thou art, <u>and that Thou art</u> a rewarder of them that diligently seek Thee.

We confess with shame that hitherto we have been lacking in that faith, without which it is impossible to please Thee; that we have been backward to discern and acknowledge Thee by reason of the blindness of our minds; and that an evil heart of unbelief has led us to distrust and depart from the living God.

Pardon, we beseech Thee, for the sake of Thy beloved Son, whatever want of faith we have shown towards Thee; and teach us henceforth by the grace of Thy Holy Spirit to trust in Thee with all our heart. Help us to set Thee always before us, so that, amidst all adversities and trials, we may steadfastly endure as seeing Thee who art invisible. Dispose us to cast upon Thee all our care, and to look to Thee for the supply of all our need, in the full persuasion that Thou carest for us and wilt not withhold from us any good thing. Above all, teach us unfeignedly to rest on the merits and grace of Thine only-begotten Son, who bore our sins in His own body on the tree, and who ever liveth to make intercession for us. And forasmuch as Thou hast given us in Christ Jesus exceeding great and precious promises, grant that we, being persuaded of them and embracing them, may confess that we are strangers and pilgrims on the earth, desiring a better country, that is an heavenly; and may be enabled to bear patiently every sorrow, to discharge faithfully every duty, and to resist firmly every temptation, while we look, not at the things which are seen and temporal, but at the things which are unseen and eternal.

Impart the like precious faith to our beloved friends. Increase everywhere the number of Thy faithful people. Encourage all who are in trouble or affliction to put their trust under the shadow of Thy wings. And let it be the comfort of the dying to know that their Redeemer liveth, and that because He liveth they shall live also.

Grant to us this day Thy favour and protection. Shield us from all evil; keep us from all sin. Enable us to confide in Thy sure promise, that as our day so shall our strength be. Guide us by thy counsel while we live, and afterward receive us into glory; through Jesus Christ, our Lord.—Amen.

Tuesday Evening.

ALMIGHTY GOD, who hast given us in Christ Jesus exceeding great and precious promises, both for the life that now is and for that which is to come, enable us to set our hope in Thee. Cause us to be persuaded in our hearts, that what Thou hast promised Thou wilt certainly perform; and that nothing is either too great for Thy power, or too good for Thy love to bestow on them that trust in Thee. And though we are not worthy of the least of all Thy mercies, yet let it please Thee, for the sake of Thy beloved Son, in whom we have redemption through His blood, to lift upon us the light of Thy countenance, and to seal us with that Holy Spirit of promise which is the earnest of our inheritance, that we may be filled with all joy and peace in believing, and may abound in hope through the power of the Holy Ghost.

O God, who hast assured us in Thy Word, that in due season we shall reap if we faint not, suffer us not to grow weary in well-doing, or to be cast down by trials and afflictions. But grant that we may be encouraged by Thy promises both to do and to suffer Thy holy will in all things, while we reckon our toils and sufferings for the present unworthy to be compared with the glory which shall be revealed in us.

Give us grace, whereby we may be enabled to hold fast the confidence and rejoicing of our hope firm unto the end. Though storms of adversity should gather around us on every side, let this hope be as an anchor of our souls, both sure and steadfast. And when the time of our departure is at hand, grant that we may commit to

Thee our spirits, in sure and certain hope of eternal life which Thou hast promised through Jesus Christ, our Saviour.

Hear our intercessions, we beseech Thee, for those whom we ought to remember in our prayers.

[Bestow Thy blessing on the children of this family. Guide them in the ways of godliness; and satisfy them early with Thy mercy, that they may rejoice and be glad all their days. Be gracious to the servants of this household. Enable them to show all good fidelity in their appointed station; and whatsoever they do, dispose them to do it heartily, as unto the Lord, and not unto men.]

Extend Thy favour to our relatives and friends. Grant that they may prosper, and be in health; above all, that their souls may prosper. Impart consolation and good hope through grace, to the sick, the dying, and all who are in trouble. And hasten the time when men in every place shall be blessed with the joys and comforts of Thy Gospel.

[And now, O God, we beseech Thee to watch over us. and over all who are dear to us, this night Suffer no evil to befall us, nor any plague to come nigh our dwelling; and, if it please Thee, raise us on the morrow to enjoy the blessings and discharge the duties of another day.]

These our humble supplications we present in the name and through the mediation of Jesus Christ, our Lord and Saviour.—Amen.

Wednesday Morning.

O GOD, who art very pitiful and of tender mercy; who regardest the poor, upliftest the downcast, and art kind even to the unthankful and the evil; dispose us heartily to acknowledge Thy goodness, and trustfully to commit ourselves to Thy care.

Enter not into judgment with Thy servants for those unnumbered shortcomings and sins, whereby we have grievously provoked Thee to hide Thy face and withdraw Thy mercies from us. Bestow upon us, for Christ's sake, Thy forgiveness. Continue to us, notwithstanding our unworthiness, the bounties of Thy providence, and the riches of Thy grace; and teach us to show our gratitude for Thy benefits, not only by the praises of our lips, but by the devoted obedience of our lives.

Help us, in imitation of Thy goodness, to be loving, generous, and compassionate towards our fellow-men. Deliver us from all selfish affections, and from all malignant and uncharitable dispositions. Suffer us not to despise any for their low estate, or to hate any for their injurious conduct, or to judge harshly of any for their infirmities and errors; but make us kindly affectioned toward all, bearing their burdens, ministering to their wants, pitying their distresses, forgiving their provocations, and doing them good as we have opportunity.

Specially grant that our love may be increased toward those that are of the household of faith. Teach us to delight in them as the excellent ones of the earth; to deal kindly with them, because Thou hast a favour to them; to honour and esteem them as bearing Thine image; and heartily to love them as those whom the

Saviour loves, and whom He requires us to love for His sake.

Graciously hear us, O God, while we plead with Thee for all whom we ought to remember at the throne of grace. Bless our friends; reward our benefactors; forgive our enemies, and enable us from the heart to forgive them. Provide for the necessities of the poor. Impart relief and comfort to the afflicted. Incline those that are rich in this world to be ready to distribute and willing to communicate; and those who are strong to bear the infirmities of the weak. Look with favour on the rising generation; and satisfy them early with Thy mercy, that they may rejoice and be glad all their days. Lift up those who are bowed down with age; and though their outward man perish, let their inward man be renewed day by day. Unite all Christians in the bonds of a common faith, and dispose them to love one another out of a pure heart fervently. Have mercy on all men; reclaim them from their errors; save them from their miseries; cleanse them from their sins; and bring them to the faith and obedience of the Gospel.

And now, O our God, we commit ourselves to Thee. Aid us this day in our several occupations. Teach us, in our intercourse with our brethren, to walk in love as Christ also loved us. And whatsoever we would that men should do unto us, help us to do even so to them.

Grant these requests, O Father, we beseech Thee, and all other things which Thou knowest to be needful for us, through Jesus Christ, our Saviour.—Amen.

Wednesday Evening.

ALMIGHTY GOD, who alone canst quiet and comfort the hearts of them that seek Thee, incline Thine ear to the voice of our supplications, and grant unto us an answer of peace. Although we have grievously provoked Thee to be angry with us, and can do nothing to appease Thy just displeasure, yet do we beseech Thee, for the sake of Thy beloved Son, on whom was laid the chastisement of our peace, to show Thy mercy upon us, and freely to forgive our manifold offences. Let not the thought of Thy wrath and the terror of Thy judgments distract or overwhelm us. Save us also from the perilous delusion of seeking peace in forgetting or forsaking Thee. Cause us to hear the voice of the Redeemer inviting the heavy-laden to come to Him, that they may find rest unto their souls. Enable us to flee for refuge to the hope set before us in the Gospel, so that we may have strong consolation. And grant that, being justified by faith, we may have peace with Thee through our Lord Jesus Christ, and may ever joy in Thee through Him by whom we have received the atonement.

Lead us also, by the guidance of Thy Holy Spirit, to walk in the ways of Thy commandments, and cause us to delight in them as ways of pleasantness and paths of peace. Deliver us from anxious cares, unruly passions, and covetous affections, whereby our hearts might be disquieted within us. And teach us, in all outward troubles which may assail us, to look up to Thee as our very present help, and to rest with unfaltering trust in Thy promise, that Thou wilt keep him in perfect peace, whose mind is stayed on Thee.

And now, O God, we humbly commit ourselves, and all whom we love, to Thy fatherly protection. Pardon all the sins of the past day, and give us grace that we may heartily repent of them. Grant us quiet sleep, and wake us on the morrow with renewed strength for the duties which await us.

Bestow, we pray Thee, the consolations of Thy grace on all who are in adversity or affliction. Impart the joy of Thy salvation to those who are in bitterness for their sins. Speak peace to them that are afar off, and bring them nigh, through the blood of Christ.

Graciously hear our humble supplications. And let the peace of God, which passeth all understanding, keep our hearts and minds, through Jesus Christ; to whom, with Thee and with the Holy Spirit, be glory everlasting. —Amen.

Thursday Morning.

ALMIGHTY GOD, who hast made the light of another day to shine upon us, we give Thee thanks for that better light of Thy glorious Gospel, wherewith Thou hast visited us, to enlighten them that were sitting in the shadow of death, and to guide our feet into the way of peace.

Help us, we beseech Thee, as children of the day, to renounce the hidden things of dishonesty, and to have no fellowship with the unfruitful works of darkness. And enable us, by walking before Thee in all holy conversation and godliness, to adorn the doctrine of God our Saviour, and to be faithful followers of Thy Son, whom Thou hast sent to be the Light of the world.

O God, who hast not appointed us to wrath, but to obtain salvation by our Lord Jesus Christ, who died for us, that, whether we wake or sleep, we should live together with Him; give us grace that we may be conformed to Him in all the virtues of His holy and blessed life, so that, by now resembling Him on earth, we may be prepared for dwelling with Him in heaven. Make us willing to take His yoke upon us, and to learn of Him who was meek and lowly in heart. And teach us, after His example, to walk in love; to go about doing good; to bear patiently all manner of evil and injurious treatment, to which we may be subjected in Thy service; and to show that our meat is to do Thy will and finish Thy work.

Pardon, O Lord, our manifold shortcomings in these things during the time that is past. Help us for the future more earnestly to look unto Jesus, that we may be changed into His image from glory to glory. And grant that we may all come into the unity of the faith and of the knowledge of the Son of God, unto a perfect man, unto the measure of the stature of the fulness of Christ.

Graciously hear us, O God, while we plead with Thee, not for ourselves only, but also for our brethren. Our heart's desire and prayer is, that they may be saved. Bring all such as are in unbelief or error to a faithful reception of the truth as it is in Jesus. And enable all professing Christians to show that the mind which was in Christ is also in them, by striving so to walk even as He walked. Specially give unto Thine afflicted servants a spirit of meek submission to Thy will, and dispose them patiently to bear their cross and to follow Christ.

[Bestow Thy blessing on the children of this family, and cause them to grow in grace as they grow in years. Regard with favour the servants of this house, and enable them, in their appointed station, faithfully to serve and honour Thee, their Master in heaven.]

And now, O our God, we humbly commit ourselves, and all whom we love, to Thy guidance and protection. Shield us from all danger; keep us from all sin. Aid us in our lawful occupations. And whatsoever we do, in word or deed, dispose us to do all in the name of the Lord Jesus, through whom we humbly offer our supplications, and to whom, with Thee and with the Holy Spirit, be glory everlasting.—Amen.

Thursday Evening.

ALMIGHTY GOD, whose eye is ever upon us, discerning not only our outward actions, but the inmost thoughts and intents of our hearts, we humble ourselves before Thee this evening, under a deep sense of our unworthiness, and earnestly seek Thy mercy to forgive us all our sins, and Thy grace effectually to cleanse us from them.

Pardon, we beseech Thee, for the sake of Thy beloved Son, whatever evil we have done, or said, or thought this day. And enable us, for the time to come, to be watchful and jealous over ourselves with a godly jealousy, lest in anything we dishonour and displease Thee, from whom our most secret trespasses cannot be hid.

Suffer us not any longer to walk in the ways of our own heart, and in the sight of our own eyes, fulfilling the desires of the flesh and of the mind. Teach us to deny ourselves, and to take up our cross daily, as faithful followers of Thy dear Son, who pleased not Himself, but cheerfully submitted to shame and suffering and death on our behalf. Make us willing, after His example, that Thy will, and not our own, should be done; and ready at His call to endure the loss of all things. Teach us to control and govern our affections, and to use a wise abstinence even from things lawful, that earthly things may not obtain dominion over us, but that we may have strength to withstand when we are tempted. And enable us to lay aside every weight, and the sin which doth so easily beset us, and to run with patience the race that is set before us, looking unto Jesus, the Author and Finisher of the Faith, who, for the joy that was set before

Him, endured the cross, despising the shame, and is set down at the right hand of the throne of God.

Father of mercies, we give Thee hearty thanks for the goodness Thou hast this day bestowed upon us; and we humbly commit ourselves, and all whom we love, to Thy fatherly care this night. Let Thine all-seeing eye watch over us, and Thine everlasting arms be underneath us.

We pray for our relatives and friends, that it may please Thee to remember them with the favour that Thou bearest unto Thy people, and to visit them with Thy salvation.

Stir up the hearts of parents and heads of families to command their children and their households after them, that they keep Thy way and observe Thine ordinances. And grant that those who are subject to their authority may willingly join with them in honouring and serving Thee.

We pray for the sick, the sorrowful, and the dying, that it may please Thee to comfort and support them, and to grant them a happy deliverance out of all their troubles.

Bless and long preserve our gracious Sovereign. Extend Thy favour and protection to our country. Further the peace and welfare of all nations. And hasten the time when all the kingdoms of the world shall become the kingdoms of our Lord and of His Christ.

Give ear, O God, to our humble supplications, which we offer in the name of Thy well-beloved Son, to whom, with Thee and with the Holy Spirit, be glory everlasting. —Amen.

Friday Morning.

ALMIGHTY GOD, the source of all goodness, who art always more ready to hear than we are to pray, and art able to do for us above all that we ask or think; we cast ourselves on Thy fatherly care, and look up to Thee for the supply of all our wants.

We confess, O God, that we know not what portion of earthly blessings may be suitable or expedient for us. Nor do we presume to ask of Thee great things. Feed us with food convenient for us. Bless us with health of body and soundness of mind. Endue us with skill, and strength, and industry, to provide for ourselves and for those who are dependent on us. Further our lawful undertakings with Thy help and blessing, and grant us such success as seemeth good in Thy sight.

Give us grace also, whereby we may be enabled to leave all our concerns to Thy disposal. Confirm our trust in the promise Thou hast given us, that they who seek the Lord shall not lack any good thing. Teach us to see in the unspeakable gift of Thy beloved Son, whom Thou hast delivered up for us all, a sure pledge that, with Him, all things shall be freely given us which Thy wisdom seeth to be truly for our good. And suffer us not to doubt that Thou, who art reserving a glorious inheritance for Thy people in the life to come, wilt faithfully provide such help, and sustenance, and comfort as are needful on their way to it.

Father of mercies, we yield Thee hearty thanks for all the benefits, temporal and spiritual, which it hath pleased Thee hitherto to bestow upon us. Pardon, for Christ's sake, wherein we have offended Thee by ungratefully forgetting or sinfully abusing them. And enable us henceforth, by the grace of Thy Holy Spirit, more thankfully to acknowledge them as Thy gifts, and more diligently to use them for Thy glory.

[O God, our Creator and Preserver, who givest food to all flesh, making the grass to grow for cattle and herbs for the service of man, regard our land, we beseech Thee, with Thy mercy, and bless us with favourable weather and fruitful seasons, that our garners may be filled with all manner of store, and our souls may have cause to rejoice in Thy bounty.]

We pray, not only for ourselves, but for our fellow-men, that it may please Thee to supply all their need according to Thy riches in glory by Christ Jesus. Provide for the poor; instruct the ignorant; reclaim the erring; comfort the sorrowful; relieve the sick; support the dying, and prepare them for their change. Extend Thy mercy to the whole human race; promote their peace, their liberty, their happiness, and bring them to the faith and obedience of Thy Gospel.

These, our humble supplications, we present in the name of Jesus, Thy beloved Son, our only Mediator.— Amen.

Friday Evening.

O GOD, who by Thy watchful providence hast upheld and guided us throughout the past day, and brought us in the enjoyment of many mercies to the close of it; we lift up our souls to Thee, in humble and hearty acknowledgment of Thy goodness.

We thank Thee for the preservation of our lives, and for the bountiful supply of our wants; for health of body and soundness of mind; for strength and skill to labour in our appointed callings, and for any measure of success with which our efforts have been crowned; for the portion of earthly good Thou hast allotted to us; for the fellowship and kindness of beloved friends, with whom Thou hast connected us in the bonds of affection; for the goodly land of light, and peace, and liberty, in which Thou hast cast our lot; and for all our temporal comforts and enjoyments.

Above all, we magnify Thy name for Thine unspeakable mercy to our souls. We thank Thee, that Thou hast so loved us, as to give Thine only-begotten Son for our redemption; that Thou hast promised through Him to bestow upon us the enlightening and sanctifying grace of Thy Holy Spirit; that Thou hast called us to the knowledge of Thy Word, which is able to make us wise unto salvation; that Thou hast borne with us long and patiently, amidst our manifold sins and provocations; that Thou hast begotten us again unto a lively hope by the resurrection of Jesus Christ from the dead, and hast taught us to look for an inheritance in heaven, that is incorruptible, undefiled, and that fadeth not away.

These benefits, O most merciful Father, we acknowledge ourselves to have received of Thine unmerited goodness. We confess that we are not worthy of the least of them. And we beseech Thee, for Thy dear Son's sake, to pardon all our ingratitude and forgetfulness, whereby we have provoked Thee to withdraw Thy tender mercies from us. Give us grace also, whereby we may be enabled more worthily to requite Thy benefits, by heartily loving Thee, confidently trusting in Thee, and cheerfully yielding up ourselves to Thy service.

To Thy fatherly care and kindness we commit ourselves, beseeching Thee, who hast blessed us hitherto, to bless us still. Remember us, and all who are dear to us, with the favour which Thou bearest unto Thy people. Supply all our need out of Thy fulness; and make all grace abound toward us, that we always, having sufficiency in all things, may abound unto every good work.

We pray, not only for ourselves, but for our fellow-creatures, that it may please Thee to succour and relieve them according to their several necessities. Have mercy on those who are sitting in darkness, and bring them to the knowledge and obedience of Thy truth. Look down from the height of Thy sanctuary on the sick, the destitute, the sorrowful, and the dying. Give them support and comfort in their affliction, and in Thy good time deliverance out of all their troubles.

Merciful Father, who givest Thy beloved sleep, let our rest this night be quiet and refreshing. And, if it please Thee, spare us to the morrow, that we may, with renewed vigour, do Thee faithful service.

Graciously hear us, for the sake of Thy beloved Son, to whom, with Thee and with the Holy Spirit, be honour and glory, world without end.—Amen.

Saturday Morning.

O GOD, who hast taught us to ask, that we may receive; to seek, that we may find; and to knock, that it may be opened unto us; incline Thine ear, we beseech Thee, to our supplications; and enable us, with the confidence of Thy children, to spread out before Thee the desires of our hearts.

We are unworthy, O Lord, that Thou shouldst regard us, by reason of our manifold offences. But in the name of Jesus, Thy beloved Son, we are encouraged to approach Thy throne of grace. And most humbly do we beseech Thee, for His sake, to pardon our sins, to purify our hearts, to help our infirmities, and to work in us that which is well-pleasing in Thy sight.

Almighty God, who in Thy wise counsels hast ordered all the circumstances of our lot, and determined the bounds of our habitation, help us to occupy contentedly and faithfully the station which Thy providence hath assigned to us. Fit us for the discharge of its duties. Strengthen us for the endurance of its trials. Guard us against its dangers and temptations. Dispose us to improve the opportunities which it affords us of glorifying Thee, and of doing good to our fellow-men. Suffer us not to walk disorderly, neglecting our own proper calling, and busying ourselves in other men's matters. But grant that it may be our study, at all times, to be quiet, and to do our own business, and to work with our own hands, as Thou hast appointed us. And enable us to render unto all their dues; fear to whom fear, honour to whom honour, tribute to whom tribute, service to whom service is due; exercising ourselves to have always a conscience void of offence toward God and toward men.

Keep us ever mindful, we beseech Thee, that we have higher duties to discharge, and more important interests to promote, than those which pertain to our present condition. Grant that, while we are not slothful in business, we may always be fervent in spirit, serving the Lord; and that, amidst our labours for the meat which perisheth, we may ever, and above all, be labouring for that meat which endureth unto everlasting life.

We implore Thy blessing on the members of this household. Give grace to all of us to discharge our relative duties with uprightness, fidelity, and diligence. Make us kindly affectioned one to another; and enable us to show how good and pleasant it is for brethren to dwell together in unity.

Bless our Sovereign, and all in authority over us, and enable them to rule in Thy fear. Bless all ranks and conditions of men throughout the land. Help them, in their several stations, faithfully to walk with Thee, and to lead a quiet life, in godliness and honesty. Promote the peace and welfare of our country. And further the enlightenment and conversion of all nations.

Father of mercies, have pity on the afflicted. Enable them to glorify Thee by a meek and trustful submission to Thy will; and let Thy chastening, though for the present not joyous but grievous, yield in them afterward the peaceable fruits of righteousness.

Graciously hear us, O God, and have mercy on us, through Jesus Christ, our Saviour.—Amen.

Saturday Evening.

ALMIGHTY GOD, our heavenly Father, we bless Thee that, by Thy good hand upon us, we have been brought safely to the close of another week, and that we are now permitted to lay ourselves down to sleep, in hope of another return of Thy sacred day. Help us, we beseech Thee, to look back with gratitude on all the aid and countenance Thou hast given us, throughout the past week, in our several occupations. And while we rejoice in the prospect of an earthly Sabbath, wherein we may cease for a season from our daily toils, dispose us, with hope and joy, to look beyond it to the everlasting rest which remaineth for Thy people.

O God, we thank Thee for the assurance Thou hast given us, that if our earthly house of this tabernacle were dissolved, we have a building of God, an house not made with hands, eternal in the heavens. Enable us, by the grace of Thy Holy Spirit, to walk by faith, not by sight, and to look, not at the things which are seen and temporal, but at the things which are unseen and eternal. Pardon wherein we have walked unworthily of the hope which is laid up for us in heaven. And grant that henceforth we may be enabled to confess that we are strangers and pilgrims on the earth, and to declare plainly, not with our lips only, but by our lives, that we are seeking a better country. Forbid that our hearts should at any time be overcharged with the cares, and riches, and pleasures of this life. Let it be our chief concern to lay up treasure in heaven. Vouchsafe to grant us, through Thy Spirit abiding in us, such present earnests and foretastes of the promised bliss, as shall cause us to esteem all earthly joys as less than nothing and vanity in comparison with it. And lead us ever onward in Thy ways, until, having gone from strength to strength, we appear, every one of us, before Thee in the heavenly Zion.

To Thy care, O God, we commend ourselves this night. Shield us from all evil. Grant us quiet sleep. And wake us on the morrow, with hearts rightly disposed to enjoy the privileges and discharge the duties of Thy Sabbath.

We pray for the several members of this family, and for all who by the ties of kindred are connected with us, that they may be blessed with Thy favour, which is better than life.

We pray for the children of adversity and affliction, that it may please Thee to succour and relieve them according to their several necessities. Be a father to the orphan, and a judge to the widow, a friend to the stranger, and a refuge to the helpless. Relieve the sick. Comfort the sorrowful. Have mercy on those who are drawing near to death. Let Thy presence sustain them, when heart and flesh are failing. And when they are absent from the body, grant that they may be present with the Lord.

We pray for the whole human race, that it may please Thee to make Thy ways known unto them, and to show Thy saving health among all nations. Turn men everywhere from darkness unto light, and from the power of Satan unto Thee, that they may receive forgiveness of their sins, and inheritance among them that are sanctified.

Give ear, we pray Thee, to our humble supplications, which we offer in the name of Thine only-begotten Son, our Lord and Saviour.—Amen.

FOURTH WEEK.

Lord's Day Morning.

O THOU that dwellest in the heavens, unto Thee we lift up our souls. Dispose us, on this day of rest, which Thou hast hallowed, to give Thee the glory due unto Thy name, and to worship Thee in the beauty of holiness. And seeing we have a great High Priest, who is touched with the feeling of our infirmities, and who ever liveth to make intercession for us, enable us through Him to come boldly unto the throne of grace, that we may obtain mercy, and find grace to help in time of need.

Great art Thou, O God, and greatly to be praised; Thy greatness is unsearchable. Thou, even Thou, art Lord alone: Thou hast made the heaven of heavens, with all their hosts; the earth and seas, and all that is therein; and Thou preservest them all; and the host of heaven worshippeth Thee. Great and marvellous are Thy works, Lord God Almighty; just and true are Thy ways, Thou King of saints. Who shall not fear Thee, O Lord, and glorify Thy name? for Thou only art holy.

Wherewith shall we come before the Lord, or bow ourselves before the High God? We confess that we are unworthy to approach Thee. For we are sinful creatures, born in corruption, prone to do evil, unable of ourselves to do good. We have broken Thy holy laws, times and ways without number. We have been unthankful for Thy benefits. We have slighted the calls and promises of Thy Word. We have turned a deaf ear to Thy warnings and admonitions. We have loved the creature more than the Creator. We have sought the possessions of earth more than the glories of heaven. We have walked according to the course of this world, and have fulfilled the desires of our own evil hearts.

Almighty God, Father of our Lord Jesus Christ, who desirest not the death of a sinner, but rather that he turn from his wickedness and live, have mercy on us according to Thy loving-kindness, and according to the multitude of Thy tender mercies blot out our transgressions.

O Son of God, Redeemer of the world, who hast loved us, and given Thyself for us, show us Thy mercy, and grant us Thy salvation. Wash us from all our sins in Thy precious blood, and through Thine intercession save us to the uttermost.

O Blessed Spirit, the Comforter and Sanctifier, let Thy grace be shed abroad in our hearts. Convince us of sin, and bring us to repentance. Enlighten our minds in the knowledge of Thy truth. And enable us to take unto our own souls those gracious promises which are given us in Christ Jesus, that we may be filled with all joy and peace in believing, and may abound in hope through the power of the Holy Ghost.

Holy, holy, holy Lord of Hosts, of whose glory the whole earth is full, enable us to glorify Thee in our body and in our spirit, which are Thine. Grant that Thy grace which hath appeared unto all men bringing salvation, may teach us to deny ungodliness and worldly lusts, and to live soberly, righteously, and godly in this present world. And dispose us steadfastly to look for that blessed hope, even the glorious appearing of the great God and our Saviour Jesus Christ, who gave Himself for us, that He might redeem us from all iniquity, and purify unto Himself a peculiar people, zealous of good works.

We thank Thee, O God, that Thou hast spared us to see another return of Thy sacred day. And we implore the aid of Thy grace to fit us for the solemn and profitable observance of it. Deliver us, we beseech Thee, from vain thoughts, distracting cares, and worldly imaginations. Preserve us from formality and insincerity, from heedlessness and levity, from unbelief and hardness of heart. And keep us in Thy fear all the day long.

Vouchsafe Thy gracious presence this day unto all the worshipping assemblies of Thy people. And enable Thy ministering servants faithfully and earnestly to declare Thy blessed Word.

Draw near to such as are necessarily withheld by sickness or affliction from worshipping in Thy courts. Hear Thou their prayers in the solitude of their dwellings, and give them the consolations of Thy grace.

Have pity on those who are wandering in error, or sitting in darkness, or hardening themselves in sin. Cause Thy marvellous light to shine upon them, and grant them repentance to the acknowledgment of the truth.

Graciously hear us, O God, and have mercy upon us, through Jesus Christ, our Saviour.—Amen.

Lord's Day Evening.

ALMIGHTY GOD, who dwellest on high, receiving the pure and perfect worship of the hosts of heaven, incline Thine ear to the praises and supplications, which, in the name of Jesus, we offer at Thy throne. Let our prayer be set forth before Thee as incense, and the lifting up of our hands as the evening sacrifice.

Thou art worthy, O Lord, to receive glory, and honour, and power; for Thou hast created all things, and for Thy pleasure they are and were created. The heavens declare Thy glory; the firmament showeth Thy handiwork; day unto day uttereth speech, night unto night showeth knowledge. O Lord, how manifold are Thy works! In wisdom hast Thou made them all. All Thy works shall praise Thee, and Thy saints shall bless Thee.

O God, who, though unseen by mortal eye, hast never left Thyself without witness, but hast caused the invisible things of Thine eternal power and Godhead to be understood through the things which Thou hast made, we thank Thee for that more perfect revelation of Thy character and will, which Thou hast given us in Thy Word. We bless Thee for those things which were written aforetime by holy men of God for our learning, that we, through patience and comfort of the Scriptures, might have hope. But above all, we magnify Thy name, that Thou, who at sundry times and in divers manners didst speak in time past unto the fathers by the prophets, hast in these last days spoken to us by Thy Son, the brightness of Thy glory, and the express image of Thy person, whom Thou hast sent to be the Light of the world.

Glory be to Thee, O God, that through Thy tender mercy the Dayspring from on high hath visited us, to give light to them that sit in darkness and in the shadow of death, and to guide our feet into the way of peace. Suffer us not to receive Thy grace in vain. But shine into our hearts, we beseech Thee, by Thy Holy Spirit, that we, being filled with the knowledge of Thy will, and animated with the hope of Thy promises, may in all things adorn the doctrine of our Saviour, and walk worthy of God, who hath called us unto His kingdom and glory.

Graciously pardon, for the sake of Thy beloved Son, our past abuse of the privileges Thou hast conferred upon us. Cast us not off as unprofitable servants. Cut us not down as cumberers of the ground. But of Thy great mercy lengthen our day of grace. Continue to us our advantages and opportunities. And enable us henceforth more justly to value them, and with greater care and diligence to profit by them, that they may not rise up in the judgment to condemn us.

Be pleased, O God, to follow with Thy rich blessing the instructions which have this day been delivered to us. Graciously receive the praises we have offered to Thee. Vouchsafe a favourable answer to our prayers. And grant that all the services of our earthly Sabbaths may, by Thy grace, prepare us for the enjoyment of the eternal Sabbath, which awaits Thy people in heaven.

Hear our intercessions, we beseech Thee, in behalf of all our brethren of mankind. Be pleased to make known the way of salvation to all who are yet in ignorance or error, and to hasten the time when the lost sheep of the house of Israel, together with the fulness of the Gentiles, shall be brought into the fold of the great Shepherd. Be very gracious to Thy servants who have gone forth to preach, whether among Jews or Gentiles, the unsearchable riches of Christ. Aid them in their labours; counsel them in their difficulties; defend them in their dangers; support them in their discouragements; and crown their efforts with abundant and increasing success.

Bless Thy whole Church; heal its divisions; reform its errors; cleanse it from its corruptions. Give grace to those who serve Thee in the Ministry, that they may be faithful and zealous in their great work, watching for souls as those who must give an account. And grant that all professing Christians may be enabled to show the sincerity of their profession by a holy practice. Stir up the hearts of Christian parents to give heed to the godly training of their families: And grant that their children, nurtured in Thy fear, may steadfastly walk in the way of Thy commandments.

Father of mercies, extend Thy compassion to all whom Thou hast visited with affliction. Give them support and comfort in their trials. And let Thy fatherly chastening be conducive to the everlasting welfare of their souls.

And now, O God, we humbly commit ourselves, and all our beloved friends, to Thy care, beseeching Thee to defend us this night from all evil, and to bring us in safety to the light of a new day.

Graciously hear the voice of our supplications, which we offer in the name of Thy well-beloved Son our Lord and Saviour.—Amen.

Monday Morning.

ALMIGHTY GOD, the source of all blessedness, in whose favour is life, and in whose presence is fulness of joy; inspire us with earnest longings for Thy fellowship, that our souls may thirst for Thee, as in a dry land where no water is, to see Thy power and Thy glory, so as we have seen Thee in the sanctuary.

We confess, O God, that our hearts have been estranged from Thee; that we have erred and strayed from Thy ways; that we have been prone to live without Thee in the world; and that by our manifold sins we have provoked Thee to cast us away from Thy presence, and to withhold Thy tender mercies from us.

Have pity on us, for the sake of Thy beloved Son, in whom Thou art always well pleased. Put not away Thy servants in anger. Leave us not, neither forsake us, O God of our salvation. Draw nigh to us, and bring us nigh to Thee. And make us glad with the light of Thy countenance.

Give us grace, whereby we may be enabled in all our ways to acknowledge Thee. Help us to live as a people who are near to Thee. Teach us to look to Thee as our very present help, and to cleave to Thee as our only satisfying portion. Be with us, O Father, everywhere, and at all times; in health or in sickness, in prosperity or in trouble, in all events and circumstances of our life; that Thy presence may sweeten and sanctify whatever befalls us. And cease not to guide and uphold us on our way, until Thou hast safely brought us to Thy heavenly kingdom, where we shall see Thee, and dwell with Thee for ever.

We give Thee thanks for the rest of the past night, and for the renewed mercies of another day. Let Thy presence go with us, and Thy grace be helpful to us, amidst all the duties or trials which now await us. Enable us to prosecute the labours of the week in the spirit of those holy services in which we were yesterday privileged to join, and of those words of heavenly truth to which we then listened. And whatsoever we are called to do, dispose us to do it heartily, not with eye-service as pleasing men, but with singleness of heart as unto Thee.

Extend, we pray Thee, the joy of Thy favour, and the comfort of Thy fellowship, to all our beloved friends. Hide not Thy face from those who are in trouble. Speak peace to them that are afar off. Reclaim the erring. And bring men everywhere to know Thee, love Thee, and trust in Thee with all their heart.

These, our humble supplications, we present to Thee in the name of Jesus, Thy beloved Son, our Lord and Saviour.—Amen.

Monday Evening.

O GOD, who knowest the secrets of every heart, and understandest our thoughts afar off; humble us under a sense of our unworthiness; and graciously pardon, for Christ's sake, our offences, which are all naked and open in Thy sight.

Who, O God, can understand his errors? Cleanse Thou us from secret faults. Keep back Thy servants also from presumptuous sins, and let them not have dominion over us. Search us, O God; and know our hearts; try us, and know our thoughts; and see if there be any wicked way in us, and lead us in the way everlasting.

Suffer us not, we beseech Thee, to delude ourselves with vain imaginations of our own excellence and sufficiency. Cause us to see ourselves as Thou seest us. Discover to us our infirmities and besetting sins. Show us what Thou knowest to be wanting in us of the faith and love and obedience which Thou requirest. Enable us impartially to examine ourselves in the light of Thy holy Word. And make us always willing to come to the light; that our deeds, if evil, may be reproved; and if good, may be made manifest that they are wrought in God. Teach us to observe with care wherein we have at any time been ensnared or overcome by the allurements of sin. Give us wisdom to mark the beginnings of evil; to avoid every scene of temptation or occasion of falling; and never to despise little things, lest we fall unawares by little and little. And while we watch, dispose us also to pray, lest we enter into temptation. Suffer us not to trust in our own strength, which is but weakness; or in our own wisdom, which is but folly; or in our own goodness, which is as the morning cloud or early dew, that passeth away. Keep us mindful that the heart is deceitful above all things, and desperately wicked; and that even when the spirit is most willing, the flesh is weak. Teach us ever to look up to Thee for those promised aids, without which we can do nothing. And grant that, building ourselves up on our most holy faith, and praying in the Holy Ghost, we may keep ourselves in the love of God, looking for the mercy of our Lord Jesus Christ unto eternal life.

To Thy watchful providence, O God, we commit ourselves, and all who are dear to us, during the coming night. Grant us quiet sleep. And, if it please Thee, spare us to enjoy the blessings and discharge the duties of another day.

Father of mercies, we beseech Thee to have compassion on those who are tried with adversity and affliction. Provide for the destitute. Comfort the mourners. Lift up those who are bowed down with years. Relieve the sick. Spare useful lives. Support the dying, and prepare them for their change.

O God, who hast made of one blood all nations, and wouldst have all men to come to the knowledge of the truth, open, we pray Thee, a great and effectual door for the preaching of Thy blessed Gospel everywhere; and hasten the time when all the ends of the earth shall see its glorious light, and hear its joyful sound.

These, our humble supplications, we present in the name of Jesus, Thy beloved Son, to whom, with Thee and with the Holy Spirit, be glory everlasting.—Amen.

Tuesday Morning.

ALMIGHTY GOD, on whom we ever depend, and without whom we can do nothing, we lift up our souls to Thee in prayer and supplication with thanksgiving. Thou art our God, early will we seek Thee. Our voice shalt Thou hear in the morning, O Lord; in the morning will we direct our prayer to Thee, and will look up.

We give Thee thanks for the rest of the past night, and bless Thy merciful providence, which hath made us to lie down in peace, and to awake in safety. And now that the light of another day is shining on us, we humbly implore the continuance of Thy care, and yield ourselves up anew to Thy service.

Holy Father, we acknowledge that we are sinful creatures, who merit no favour or kindness at Thy hands. But putting our trust in the merits of Thy dear Son, in whom we have redemption through His blood, we pray Thee to blot out our sins from Thy remembrance; and to give us grace, that henceforth we may be enabled to glorify Thee in our body and in our spirit, which are Thine.

O God, who desirest truth in the inward parts, and unto whom no services are acceptable but such as proceed from a pure and honest heart; cast out, we pray Thee, all evil from within us. Save us from error, impenitence, and unbelief. Preserve us from that insensibility of conscience which might lead us to excuse or justify ourselves, while leading a careless, unprofitable, and godless life. Deliver us from sinful tempers, unholy thoughts, and inordinate affections; from pride, envy, covetousness, and uncharitableness. Inspire us with unfeigned love to God and to man. Teach us to maintain a constant habit of self-government; and enable us with all diligence to keep the heart, out of which are the issues of life.

Set a watch also, O Lord, before our mouth, and keep the door of our lips, that we may not sin against Thee with our tongue. Help us to repress all fretful repinings, uncharitable censures, and profane or foolish levities. Let all bitterness, and wrath, and anger, and clamour, and lying, and evil speaking, be put away from us. And grant that no corrupt communication may proceed out of our mouth, but that which is good to the use of edifying, that it may minister grace unto the hearers.

Almighty God, of whose grace alone it is that Thy people are able to do any good thing; help us in all our actions to maintain a strict regard to Thy revealed will, and carefully to shun every false and wicked way. Teach us to renounce the hidden things of dishonesty; to have no fellowship with the unfruitful works of darkness; and to abstain from all appearance of evil. Make us watchful against temptation; provident of our time; circumspect in our walk; diligent, just, and prudent in our business; temperate in our enjoyments, and patient in our trials. And whether we eat or drink, or whatsoever we do, enable us to do all to Thy glory.

Let Thy blessing rest on the inmates of this house. Give grace to all of us to discharge our several duties [as parents or children, masters or servants] with uprightness, fidelity, and diligence. Bestow Thy favour on our relatives and friends. Grant that they may prosper, and be in health; above all, that their souls may prosper. Have pity on those whom Thou has visited with affliction, and give them the consolations of Thy grace

Look in mercy on the whole race of mankind; and speedily diffuse Thy Gospel throughout the world, to enlighten and convert the nations that sit in darkness.

And now, O our God, we commit ourselves to Thee. Show us Thy ways; teach us Thy paths; lead us in Thy truth, and teach us; for Thou art the God of our salvation; on Thee would we wait all the day. Graciously hear us, and grant an answer of peace, through Jesus Christ, our Lord.—Amen.

Tuesday Evening.

ALMIGHTY and most merciful God, in whom we live and move and have our being, and by whom all the circumstances which surround us, and all the events which befall us, are determined; impress us with a sense of our dependence on Thee, and enable us to trust in Thee with all our heart.

Give us that full reliance on Thy grace, which will lead us, notwithstanding our sins, to confide in the special care and kindness of Thy providence. Teach us to know Thee as our reconciled God, whose just anger hath in Christ Jesus been turned away, and whose thoughts toward us are thoughts of peace, and not of evil. And cause us to be strengthened and comforted by the persuasion, that if Thou art for us, nothing can be against us, and that all things, how adverse soever they may appear, shall, if we love Thee, work together for our good.

Pardon, we beseech Thee, for the sake of Thy beloved Son, whatever lack of confidence we have shown in the righteousness and goodness of Thy dealings with us; and lead us henceforth, by the teaching of Thy Holy Spirit, with greater cheerfulness and steadfastness to hope in Thee. Deliver us from anxious thoughts and disquieting fears, whether for ourselves or for any who are dear to us. Suffer us not to doubt, that Thou, our heavenly Father, who clothest the grass of the field and feedest the fowls of the air, wilt much more provide for Thy children all things which Thou knowest to be necessary or expedient for them. Whatever of this world's good it may please Thee, either to give, or to withhold, or to take away; make us entirely submissive to Thy will, and trustful, even against hope, in Thine eternal love. And give us a heart always to prefer things heavenly to things earthly; that, seeking first Thy kingdom and righteousness, we may, by Thy mercy, obtain the sure promise both of the life that now is and of that which is to come.

Father of mercies, we thankfully acknowledge Thy care and kindness during the past day; and now, at the close of it, we commit ourselves to Thy keeping. We will lay ourselves down in peace and sleep, because Thou only makest us to dwell in safety.

Look with tender compassion, we beseech Thee, on all Thy people whom Thou hast visited with affliction. Help them to bow in meek submission to Thy will. And cause them to be persuaded in their hearts, that however grievous Thy chastening may seem to be, it is sent in love and fraught with mercy.

Extend Thy favour to all our brethren of mankind. Our heart's desire and prayer is, that they may be saved. Let the people praise Thee, O God; let all the people praise Thee.

[Almighty God, who givest food to all flesh, regard our land, we beseech Thee, with Thy favour. Remember Thy promise, that seed-time and harvest shall not cease while the earth remaineth, and send unto us favourable weather and fruitful seasons, that our fields may in due time yield an abundant increase, and our souls may have cause to rejoice in Thy bounty.]

Incline Thine ear, we beseech Thee, to our supplications, which we offer in the name of Thine only-begotten Son, our Lord and Saviour.—Amen.

Wednesday Morning.

O LORD our God, who dwellest in the heavens, but humblest Thyself to behold the things that are in the earth; incline Thine ear to the voice of our supplications. Although we are unworthy of Thy favour by reason of our manifold offences, yet do we beseech Thee, in the name of Thy beloved Son, to receive us graciously and to love us freely; forgiving us those things for which our own hearts condemn us, and making us glad with the light of Thy countenance. Give us grace, whereby we may be enabled to show our sense of Thine undeserved mercy, not only by love to Thee who hast first loved us, but by kind and charitable dispositions towards our brethren, and by abounding in those peaceable fruits of righteousness, which are unto Thy praise and glory, through Christ Jesus.

O God, who art ever merciful and gracious, long-suffering and slow to anger; who hast not dealt with us after our sins, nor rewarded us according to our iniquities; give unto Thy servants a meek and quiet spirit, that we may not be easily provoked by any wrongs, or quick to resent any indignities; but that we may be patient toward all men, and ready to forgive, even as Thou, for Christ's sake, forgivest us.

Dispose us, in our intercourse with our fellow-men, to shun every occasion of discord and contention. Suffer us not to be desirous of vainglory, provoking one another and envying one another. Help us to put away from us all bitterness, and wrath, and anger, and clamour, and evil speaking, with all malice. And teach us to love as brethren, to be pitiful, to be courteous, and to follow after the things which make for peace, and things wherewith one may edify another.

Grant that peace may abide in this household, and that all the members of it may dwell together in unity. Bestow Thy favour on our relatives and friends. Reward with Thy bounty all who have done us good. Forgive all who have done or wished us evil, and enable us to forgive them from the heart.

Have pity on those whom Thou hast visited with affliction. Enable them meekly to submit to Thy will; and sanctify Thy chastening for their good.

We pray for the peace and welfare of Thy whole Church, that its breaches may be healed, its errors reformed, and that all its members may stand fast in one spirit, and strive together with one mind for the faith of the Gospel.

We pray for the peace and prosperity of our native land; and for the enlightenment and conversion of all nations. Put an end, we beseech Thee, to strife and tumults, as well as to ignorance and superstition everywhere. And hasten the time, when the Prince of Peace shall take to Himself His great power, and reign over the whole earth; and when, under the benign influence of His dominion, nation shall no longer rise against nation, neither shall they learn war any more.

Graciously hear our petitions, which we offer to Thee in the name of Thy beloved Son, our Lord and Saviour. —Amen.

Wednesday Evening.

ALMIGHTY GOD, Father of mercies, who givest us richly all things to enjoy, we render praise to Thee for Thy goodness. We bless Thee, that Thou hast created us by Thy power, and hast constantly upheld and preserved us by Thy providence. But above all, we magnify Thy name, that Thou hast so loved the world, as to give Thine only-begotten Son, that whosoever believeth in Him should not perish, but have everlasting life.

Fill our hearts with gratitude, we beseech Thee, for the great love wherewith Thou hast loved us. And enable us to show our sense of it, not with our lips only, but in our lives, by presenting our bodies a living sacrifice, holy and acceptable unto Thee.

Grant also, O God, that our souls may be inspired with warm and grateful affection towards Him, who loved us and gave Himself for us. Reveal to us the excellencies of His character, and cause us to see that He is altogether lovely. Teach us to adore the wonders of His grace, in that though He was rich, yet for our sakes He became poor, that we through His poverty might be rich. Strengthen us with might by Thy Spirit in the inner man, that Christ may dwell in our hearts by faith; and that we, being rooted and grounded in love, may be able to comprehend with all saints what is the breadth, and length, and depth, and height, and to know the love of Christ, which passeth knowledge. And grant that His love may constrain us, while we thus judge, that if one died for all, then all died; and that He died for all, that they who live should not henceforth live unto themselves, but unto Him who died for them and rose again.

O God, who desirest truth in the inward parts, suffer us not to deceive our own souls, by professing much love to the Saviour, while yet in our hearts and lives we are estranged from Him. Enable us to show that we love Him in sincerity, by studying to please Him and delighting to honour Him; by doing with our might whatsoever our hand findeth to do, for the furtherance of His cause, and the benefit of His people; and by esteeming no labours burdensome, and no sacrifices grievous which He requireth of us.

Give us grace, that we may steadfastly cleave to Him, as one whom, not having seen, we love; and in whom, though now we see Him not, yet believing, we rejoice with joy unspeakable and full of glory. And grant that our love to Him may abound more and more, and that we may be led by it more and more zealously to do all things whatsoever He hath commanded us; until, having faithfully served Him on the earth, we are taken to dwell with Him eternally in heaven.

O Thou Keeper of Israel who never slumberest, watch over us this night, and keep us from all evil. Extend Thy favour and protection to our beloved friends. Regard with tender pity those who are in affliction, and overrule the trials they are enduring for the everlasting welfare of their souls. Have mercy on those who are perishing for lack of knowledge; and hasten the time when all the ends of the earth shall be brought to the faith and obedience of Thy Gospel.

Grant these requests, O God, we beseech Thee, through Jesus Christ, our Lord.—Amen.

Thursday Morning.

O LORD our God, who art not far from any one of us, and hast taught us to look to Thee as our very present help, we cast ourselves on Thy fatherly care, and humbly beseech Thee to supply all our need, according to Thy riches in glory by Christ Jesus.

Make us thankful for the rest of the past night, and for the returning light and blessings of another day. And now that Thou art calling us to resume our daily work, impress us with a sense of our dependence on Thee, and teach us faithfully to acknowledge Thee in all our ways.

Keep us ever mindful, O God, that it is our first duty to glorify and serve Thee. Cause us to feel how much we owe to Thee, as our Creator, Preserver, Benefactor, and Redeemer. Fill our hearts with such love to Thee, that nothing may seem too hard for us to do or to suffer in obedience to Thy will. And whether we eat or drink, or whatsoever we do, enable us to do all to Thy glory.

Teach us, while ever walking in Thy fear, to be just and righteous in our dealings with our brethren. Suffer us not to beguile any with deceitful words, or to injure any by wrongful or oppressive actions. Grant that integrity and uprightness may preserve us from seeking at any time the advancement of our own interests, or the relief of our own necessities, by trespassing on the rights of others. Let it be our hearty desire to render unto all their dues, and our earnest endeavour to be faithful in that which is least, as well as in that which is greatest. And let our rejoicing be the testimony of our conscience, that in simplicity and godly sincerity, not with fleshly wisdom, but by the grace of God, we have our conversation in the world.

O God, who knowest how prone we are to abuse Thy bounties to our own hurt and Thy dishonour, give us grace that we may so use the good things, which Thou hast provided for the sustenance of the body, that they may not in any wise be hurtful to the soul. Restrain us from all intemperance or excess. Enable us to be sober and vigilant, that we may keep under the body and bring it into subjection. Help us to repress all inordinate desires for the riches, honours, and pleasures of this life. And suffer us not to be forgetful of Thy solemn warning, that if we live after the flesh we shall die, but if, through the Spirit, we mortify the deeds of the body, we shall live.

Holy Father, we acknowledge that in time past we have failed to render the homage that is due to Thee; and that in many things we have come far short of the duties we owe to our fellow-creatures and to ourselves. Forgive us freely through the merits of Thy beloved Son. And give us grace, that henceforth we may be enabled to deny ourselves to all ungodliness and worldly lusts, and to lead a godly, righteous, and sober life, to the glory of Thy holy name.

Let Thy presence go with us this day to our appointed duties; and let Thy grace in all things be sufficient for us. Hear our intercessions, we beseech Thee, for all whom we ought to remember at Thy throne of grace.

We commend to Thy favour our relatives and friends. Grant that they may prosper in all things, and be in health; above all, that their souls may prosper. Reward with Thy bounty all that have done us good. Pardon and convert all that have done or wished us evil; and enable us to forgive them from the heart.

[Bestow Thy blessing on the children of this family. Keep them from the snares and dangers of an evil world; and cause them to grow in knowledge and in grace. Regard with Thy favour the servants of this household; and enable them, in their appointed station, faithfully to serve and honour Thee, their Master in heaven.]

Bless and long preserve our Sovereign. Prosper all the interests of our country. Hasten the prevalence of Thy kingdom among all nations.

God of all comfort, have pity on the afflicted. Assuage their griefs; relieve their sufferings; and overrule Thy chastening for their good. Have mercy on those who are drawing near to death. Let Thy grace sustain them when heart and flesh are failing. And when they are absent from the body, grant that they may be present with the Lord.

Graciously hear and answer us, O God, according to Thy promises made to us in Christ Jesus, to whom, with Thee and with the Holy Spirit, be glory everlasting.— Amen.

Thursday Evening.

ALMIGHTY GOD, who by Thy wise providence hast ordered all the circumstances of our lot, and crowned us with unmerited loving-kindnesses, dispose us thankfully to acknowledge Thy goodness, and humbly to submit ourselves to Thy will.

Enter not into judgment with Thy servants for the frowardness, impatience, and discontentment, wherewith we have at any time rebelled against Thee. Pardon, for Christ's sake, wherein we have offended Thee by covetous affections or repining dispositions. And give us grace, that henceforth we may be enabled to yield ourselves up entirely to Thy disposal, and with unquestioning meekness to acquiesce in the wisdom, righteousness, and goodness of Thy dealings with us.

Convince us that we are not worthy of the least of all Thy mercies, and that we have no cause to murmur, when Thy gracious gifts are denied us or withdrawn from us. Teach us to be still, and to know that Thou art God, acknowledging Thy right to do with us as seemeth good in Thy sight. Prepare us to receive evil, as well as good, at Thy hand, in the confident persuasion that Thou chastenest us, not for Thy pleasure, but for our profit, that we may be partakers of Thy holiness. And enable us to possess our souls in patience, amidst the trials and troubles of our present condition, believing that our light affliction, which is but for a moment, worketh for us a far more exceeding and eternal weight of glory.

Heavenly Father, who in Thy wisdom knowest what portion of earthly good is expedient for us, teach us, in whatsoever state we are, therewith to be content. Make us to consider that the happiness of a man's life consisteth not in the abundance of the things which he possesses, but that godliness with contentment is great gain. Teach us to count all things but loss for the excellency of the knowledge of Christ Jesus our Lord, in whom Thou hast blessed us with all spiritual and heavenly blessings. And satisfy our souls with His divine fulness, so that, whatever adversities befall us, we may be enabled cheerfully to submit to them ; as troubled, yet not distressed ; as perplexed, but not in despair ; as cast down, but not destroyed ; as sorrowful, yet alway rejoicing ; as having nothing, and yet possessing all things.

And now, O God, we commit ourselves to Thee, who hast said that Thou wilt never leave us nor forsake us. Watch over us this night ; deliver us from evil ; and grant us quiet sleep under the shadow of Thy wings.

Regard with Thy favour our family and kindred, our friends and neighbours, and all who are connected with us. Think upon them for good, and visit them with Thy salvation.

Extend Thy help and pity to the afflicted. And strengthen them with might, according to Thy glorious power, unto all patience and long-suffering with joyfulness.

Reveal Thy marvellous light to those who are in darkness. And increase everywhere the number of Thy people, who know Thy name, and put their trust in Thee.

Graciously hear our supplications, which we offer in the name of Thy beloved Son, our Lord and Saviour.— Amen.

Friday Morning.

ALMIGHTY GOD, the Author of our being; the Preserver of our lives; the Redeemer of our souls; the source of all our blessings and of all our hopes; we acknowledge Thy manifold claims to the grateful affection and obedience which Thou requirest of us, and humbly implore the grace of Thy Holy Spirit, that we may give Thee the love and homage that are due.

Whom have we, O Lord, in heaven but Thee? And there is none upon earth that we desire beside Thee. O that there were such an heart in us, that we would fear Thee, and keep all Thy commandments always, that it might be well with us and with our children for ever.

O our God, we have cause to be ashamed, that hitherto we have been so little affected by a sense of our obligation to serve Thee, and have so greatly failed in the diligence and fervour wherewith it becomes us to do Thy holy will. Pardon, we beseech Thee, for the sake of Thy beloved Son, our lack of zeal for the honour of Thy name. Enter not into judgment with Thy servants for the coldness of our affections, the fickleness of our purposes, the sluggishness and weakness of our endeavours. And give us grace, that henceforth we may be enabled to yield Thee the full devotion of our hearts, and earnestly to employ all our faculties and talents in obedience to Thy will, and in subserviency to Thy glory.

Almighty God, who workest in us to will and to do of Thy good pleasure, strengthen us with might by Thy Spirit in the inner man, that we may be ready to every good word and work. Suffer us not to grow lukewarm in Thy ways, or faint and weary in keeping Thy commandments. Inflame our hearts with such love to Thee, that nothing may seem to us too hard to do, or too grievous to suffer for Thy sake. Above all, grant that our souls may be brought under the constraining power of redeeming love, so that we may live no longer unto ourselves, but unto Him who loved us and died for us.

Giver of all good, we look up to Thee for the supply of our daily returning wants. Bestow upon us needful sustenance, and contentment therewith. And bless us in all the work of our hands. [Send unto us favourable weather and fruitful seasons, that our land may abundantly yield her increase, and our souls may have cause to rejoice and be glad in Thee.]

Aid us this day, we beseech Thee, in our several duties. And grant that we may be not slothful in business, but fervent in spirit, serving the Lord.

Bestow Thy favour and blessing on our friends. Impart consolation to all who are in sorrow. Provide for the destitute. Deliver the oppressed. Support the aged. Relieve the sick. Prepare for their departure those who are about to die.

Have pity on those who are perishing for lack of knowledge. Give to Thy Son the heathen for His inheritance, and the uttermost parts of the earth for His possession. And stir up the hearts of all professing Christians to greater zeal, liberality, and prayerfulness, in seeking the diffusion of Thy Gospel throughout the world.

Graciously hear us, for the sake of Jesus Christ, our Lord and Saviour.—Amen.

Friday Evening.

O LORD our God, Most High and Mighty, King of kings and Lord of lords, before whom all the nations of the earth are counted less than nothing and vanity; dispose us now and always to approach Thee under a just sense of Thy Majesty. Keep us mindful that Thou resistest the proud, but givest grace unto the humble. And strengthen our faith in the word which Thou hast spoken to us, that Thou, who inhabitest eternity and whose name is Holy, dwellest with him also that is of a contrite and humble spirit, to revive the spirit of the humble, and the heart of the contrite ones.

We acknowledge with shame that we have often sinned against Thee, by cherishing proud and vain imaginations, by thinking of ourselves more highly than we ought to think, and by claiming or coveting pre-eminence above our brethren.

Pardon, we beseech Thee, for the sake of Thy beloved Son, wherein we have thus, or in any way, offended Thee. And give us grace, that henceforth we may be enabled faithfully to render that which Thou requirest of us, by doing justly, loving mercy, and walking humbly with Thee our God.

Cause us, O Lord, to feel that we are nothing, and have nothing, and deserve nothing of ourselves. Convince us that every excellence or attainment, of which we are at any time inclined to boast, is truly Thy gift, for which it becomes us, instead of glorying, to own ourselves indebted to Thee. Suffer us not to be forgetful of our sins, which ought ever to fill us with shame and self-abasement. Graft in our hearts that excellent grace of charity, which vaunteth not itself, is not puffed up, and doth not behave itself unseemly; so that, in all our intercourse with our fellow-men, nothing may be done through strife or vainglory, but that each of us may in lowliness of mind esteem others better than himself. And help us to imitate the pattern of humility which our blessed Lord and Saviour hath set before us, that learning of Him who was meek and lowly in heart, we may for the present find rest unto our souls, and hereafter be honoured and exalted in His heavenly kingdom.

Bestow the like blessings, we pray Thee, on our beloved friends. Let the mind that was in Christ Jesus be found in all His people. Specially grant unto Thine afflicted servants a spirit of humble submission to Thy will. And so further the cause of pure religion throughout the world, that men everywhere may serve Thee with humility. Let not the wise man glory in his wisdom, nor the mighty man in his might, nor the rich man in his riches; but he that glorieth, let him glory in the Lord.

Father of mercies, we thankfully acknowledge Thy goodness to us throughout the past day; and we humbly commit ourselves, and all whom we love, to Thy watchful care during this night. Suffer no evil to befall us, nor any plague to come nigh our dwelling. Grant us quiet sleep, and raise us on the morrow with renewed strength for the duties which may then await us.

Hear our humble supplications, we beseech Thee, and do for us abundantly above all that we ask or think, through Jesus Christ our Saviour.—Amen.

Saturday Morning.

O GOD, we worship, and bow down; we kneel before Thee, our Lord and Maker; for Thou art our God; and we are the people of Thy pasture, and the sheep of Thy hand. We praise Thy name, that though we have often wandered from Thy ways and hardened our hearts against Thee, yet Thou art pleased to deal bountifully with us, and to crown us from day to day with undeserved benefits.

Pardon, we beseech Thee, for the sake of Thy beloved Son, our ungrateful returns for Thy manifold loving-kindnesses. Deal not with us according to our sins, whereby we have so frequently provoked Thee to withdraw Thy tender mercies from us. And give us grace, that henceforth we may be enabled to bring forth fruits meet for repentance, and to show our sense of Thy goodness by a life of cheerful obedience to Thy commandments.

Almighty God, who didst in the beginning command the light to shine out of darkness, and hast again made the light of the sun to arise upon the world in the morning of another day; let it please Thee so to illuminate our souls with the grace of Thy Holy Spirit, that we may be guided in the paths of righteousness, and brought to know Thee and Thy Son Jesus Christ, whom to know is life eternal. Deliver us, we pray Thee, from ignorance and delusion, from prejudice and passion, from pride and self-confidence,—and from every evil influence that opposes the entrance of Thy truth into our minds. Give to us humble, teachable, and obedient hearts, that we may meekly receive whatsoever Thou hast taught us. Make us ready to believe, where we cannot see: and willing to trust, where we cannot comprehend. Endue us with a right judgment in all things, that we may know the things that are true, and approve the things that are excellent. And grant that Thy truth may so richly dwell in us, in all wisdom and spiritual understanding, that by it we may be built up in holiness and comfort through faith unto salvation.

Blessed Lord, who art of power to stablish us according to Thy Gospel, hold Thou us up, that we fall not from our steadfastness. Deliver us from the instruction which causeth to err. Keep us upright among all diversities of opinions and judgments in this world, that we may not swerve from Thine eternal truth. And grant that in all perplexities and doubts we may be upheld and guided by Thy Holy Spirit. Suffer us not to be as children, tossed to and fro, and carried about with every wind of doctrine. But cause us to grow both in knowledge and in grace. And enable us to continue in the faith, grounded and settled, that we be not moved away from the hope of the Gospel.

[To Thy fatherly care and guidance we commend ourselves, amidst the duties or trials which may now await us. Remember in our behalf Thy precious promise, that as our day so shall our strength be. Cause us to hear Thy loving-kindness in the morning; for in Thee do we trust. Cause us to know the way wherein we should walk; for we lift up our souls unto Thee. Teach us to do Thy will; for Thou art our God: Thy Spirit is good; lead us into the land of uprightness.]

Graciously hear us, O God, while we plead with Thee, not for ourselves only, but also for our fellow-men. Send forth the light of Thy Gospel throughout the world, to enlighten and reclaim the nations that are in darkness. Take away from the hearts of Thine ancient people the veil that hinders them from seeing the fulfilment of Thy promises made unto their fathers. Arrest the progress of infidelity and ungodliness. Hasten the downfall of idolatry and superstition. Abolish every system of doctrine or of worship that is contrary to Thy revealed truth. And pour out Thy Holy Spirit upon all flesh, that all may know Thee, from the least unto the greatest.

We pray for the peace and welfare of Thy whole Church. Cleanse it more and more from errors and impurities. Enlighten and guide all pastors and teachers, that they may fully know and faithfully proclaim Thy Gospel. And grant that Thy professed people everywhere, being nourished in the words of faith and of good doctrine, may adorn their Christian profession by a godly life.

Father of mercies and God of all comfort, look down, we pray Thee, from the height of Thy sanctuary on the poor, the sorrowful, the sick, and the dying. Succour and relieve them according to their need. And grant that their present affliction may work for them a far more exceeding and eternal weight of glory.

Graciously hear and answer us, O Lord, according to the fulness of Thy mercy in Christ Jesus; to whom, with Thee and with the Holy Spirit, be glory everlasting.—Amen.

Saturday Evening.

ALMIGHTY and everlasting God, by whose good hand upon us we have been brought to the close of another week and the eve of another Sabbath; we give Thee thanks for the patience and forbearance which, in the time that is past, Thou hast manifested toward us, and for all the blessings, temporal and spiritual, which we have constantly received at Thy most bountiful hand. It is of Thy mercies, O Lord, that we are not consumed, because Thy compassions fail not. We have daily provoked Thee to anger with our sins, and yet Thou hast daily loaded us with benefits. We have wickedly abused the riches of Thy long-suffering, and slighted the things which belong unto our peace; and yet Thou hast mercifully lengthened our day of grace, and multiplied our opportunities of repentance.

Lord God, merciful and gracious, who desirest not the death of a sinner, but rather that he turn from his wickedness and live, incline us with all our hearts to turn unto Thee, and cause Thy face to shine, that we may be saved. Bestow upon us, through the merits of Jesus Christ, the free forgiveness of all our past sins. And enable us, by the grace of Thy Holy Spirit, to amend our lives according to Thy Word, and to bring forth abundantly those fruits of holy obedience which are, through Jesus Christ, unto the praise and glory of Thy name.

O God, who hast taught us in Thy Word, and art oftentimes reminding us by Thy providence, that it is appointed unto all men once to die, and that in the midst of life we are in death, impress us with a sense of our frailty, and so teach us to number our days, that we may apply our hearts unto wisdom. Give us grace to be watchful and prayerful, having our loins girt and our lights burning, as becometh servants waiting for their Lord, who know not the hour when He shall come. Grant that the close of every day may admonish us, that the end of all earthly things is at hand, and that we must finish the works Thou hast given us to do, before the night cometh, when no man can work. And help us by Thy grace to make our daily life a constant course of preparation for eternity; so that death may be no more a terror to our waiting souls, than sleep is to our wearied bodies, and the grave may become to us a bed of rest, from which we shall be raised to everlasting joy and glory.

[Almighty God, Father of our Lord Jesus Christ, who, by the death of Thy Son, hast destroyed death, and by His resurrection hast assured us that they also who sleep in Him shall rise again, receive our unfeigned thanks, we beseech Thee, for that victory over death and the grave which He hath achieved for us; and grant that we, while still in the body, may be kept in constant fellowship with Him who is the Resurrection and the Life; so that, when our earthly house of this tabernacle is dissolved, our souls may be received into His presence, and our flesh also may rest in hope, till this corruptible shall put on incorruption, and this mortal shall put on immortality.]

Heavenly Father, we acknowledge Thy past goodness, and humbly beseech Thee, who hast blessed us hitherto, to bless us still. Watch over us this night. Grant us refreshing sleep. Mercifully spare us to see the light of another Sabbath. And grant that we may awake with hearts duly prepared to enjoy its privileges and to discharge its solemn duties.

Graciously hear us, O God, while we plead with Thee for all conditions and classes of our fellow-men. Provide for the poor. Instruct the ignorant. Reclaim the erring. Comfort the afflicted. Be the guide of the young, and the staff of the aged; the orphan's stay, and the stranger's shield. Deliver those who are in danger or distress. Prepare for their great change those who are about to die.

Look in mercy on the whole human race. Enlighten and convert the nations that are yet in darkness. Watch over Thy flock wherever they be scattered. Gather in both Jews and Gentiles into Thy fold. And hasten the time when there shall be one fold and one Shepherd.

Hear us, O God, and graciously accept of us, through Jesus Christ, Thy well-beloved Son, to whom, with Thee and with the Holy Spirit, be all honour and glory, world without end.—Amen.

Prayers for Sacramental and other Special Occasions.

Morning of a Sacramental Fast Day.

LORD GOD, merciful and gracious, who art of purer eyes than to behold iniquity, but hast promised pardon, through Thy beloved Son, to such as truly repent and believe on Him; we humble ourselves before Thy holy presence under a deep sense of our unworthiness, and earnestly plead for mercy to forgive us, and for grace to help us according to our need.

We confess, O God, that we are fallen and sinful creatures. Our hearts are naturally corrupt and depraved; and to our original sin we have added many actual transgressions. We have broken Thy holy laws. We have been unthankful for Thy benefits. We have slighted alike the calls of Thy Word, and the chastenings and warnings of Thy providence. We have loved the creature more than the Creator, and have preferred our own ease and pleasure to Thy glory.

We acknowledge that we have sinned, not only against Thee, but also against our brethren of mankind, by pride and envy, by malice and uncharitableness, by withholding good from them when it was in our power to do it, instead of loving our neighbours as ourselves.

Nor have we been less guilty against our own souls. We have harboured evil thoughts; cherished impure affections; suffered our hearts to be overcharged with the cares, and vanities, and pleasures of this life, and neglected the things which belong unto our peace.

Behold, we are vile; what shall we answer Thee? Innumerable evils have compassed us about; our iniquities have taken hold upon us, so that we are not able to look up; they are more than the hairs of our head, therefore our heart faileth us. Be pleased, O Lord, to deliver us; O Lord, make haste to help us.

We plead Thy promise, that if we confess our sins, Thou art faithful and just to forgive them, and to cleanse us from all unrighteousness. And earnestly do we beseech Thee, for the sake of Jesus Christ our Saviour and Intercessor, to turn away from us the terrors of Thy wrath, and to bless us with the light of Thy countenance.

O most merciful God, who of Thy great love hast given Thine only-begotten Son to be the propitiation for our sins, and hast declared Thine acceptance of His sacrifice, in that Thou hast raised Him from the dead; increase, we beseech Thee, our faith in Him; and grant that Thy Holy Spirit, while convincing us of sin, may enable us to take unto our own hearts the blessed assurance of Thy forgiveness and fatherly kindness through Jesus Christ our Lord; so that we may be filled with all joy and peace in believing, and may abound in hope through the power of the Holy Ghost.

Give us grace also, whereby we may be enabled to bring forth fruits meet for repentance. Grant that, with godly sorrow for the past, and with sincere purposes of obedience for the future, we may think upon our ways, and turn our feet unto Thy testimonies, and make haste to keep Thy commandments. Bestow upon us the grace of Thy Holy Spirit, that we may be enlightened in the knowledge of Thy Word, renewed in holiness after Thine image, strengthened with all might for the doing of Thy blessed will, and made to abound more and more in the fruit of the Spirit, which is in all goodness and righteousness and truth.

We give Thee thanks for the prospect Thou art affording us of showing forth the death of our Redeemer, and partaking of the symbols of His broken body and shed blood. Aid us in all our preparatory exercises of prayer, and self-examination, and repentance. Search us, O God, and know our hearts; try us, and know our thoughts; and see if there be any wicked way in us, and lead us in the way everlasting.

Meet with us, we beseech Thee, in Thy courts, and help us to worship Thee in spirit and in truth. Enable Thy ministering servants to speak to us a word in season; and grant that their preaching may be accompanied with the demonstration and power of Thy Holy Spirit.

Let Thy Word everywhere have free course and be glorified, and hasten the time when it shall be preached throughout the whole world.

Graciously hear us, O God, and have mercy upon us, through Jesus Christ, our Saviour.—Amen.

Evening of a Sacramental Fast Day.

O THOU high and lofty One, who inhabitest eternity, whose name is Holy; look down, in the greatness of Thy compassion, on us Thine unworthy children assembled before Thee. Graciously hear the confessions and prayers which we have this day made to Thee in the name of Thy beloved Son. Work in us by the grace of Thy Holy Spirit that broken and penitent heart which Thou despisest not. And mercifully fulfil to us Thy promise, that Thou wilt not contend for ever, neither wilt Thou be always wroth, lest the Spirit should fail before Thee, and the souls which Thou hast made.

O God, with whom there is forgiveness that Thou mayest be feared, comfort our hearts, we beseech Thee, with a full persuasion of Thy fatherly mercy in Jesus Christ our Saviour; and let a sense of Thine undeserved goodness excite in us a holy dread of offending Thee, and an earnest desire in all things to obey Thee. Dispose us to love much, as becometh those to whom much hath been forgiven. Enable us to show the sincerity of our love by a cheerful and steadfast conformity to Thy commandments. And being redeemed with the precious blood of Christ, may we no longer live as if we were our own, but yield up ourselves entirely to Thy service, and glorify Thee in our body and in our Spirit, which are Thine.

We thank Thee for the prospect we now have of joining in that holy ordinance in which our Redeemer's sufferings are commemorated, and the precious blessings purchased by His death are represented and sealed to His faithful people. We acknowledge our unworthiness of so great a privilege. We look back with humiliation and regret on the many past communions we have misimproved. We deeply lament that our holy impressions at the Table of the Lord have so often been effaced, and that our solemn vows have so often been forgotten. O Lord, lay not these sins to our charge. And now that Thou art once more inviting us to sit down at Thy table, enable us to go thither with more simplicity and godly sincerity than hitherto; with a livelier faith, a warmer love, a deeper penitence; with hearts more humbly dependent on Thy grace, and more firmly devoted to Thy service.

To this end let it please Thee to bless unto us the exercises in which we have this day been engaged, and the instructions which have been addressed to us from the Scriptures. Let not Thy Word return unto Thee void. May its precious truths abide in our minds, and its holy fruits be manifest in our conduct.

And now, O God, we cast ourselves on Thy care. Watch over us during the darkness of the coming night. Grant us quiet sleep, and, if it please Thee, preserve us to see the light of another day.

Bestow Thy favour on our friends and fellow-worshippers. Cause them to see the good of Thy chosen, and visit them with Thy salvation.

Bless our Queen and all the Royal Family. Encompass them with the shield of Thy protection, and bestow upon them Thy loving-kindness, which is better than life.

Bless all ranks and conditions of men among us. Enable them faithfully to serve and honour Thee in whatsoever calling or station Thou hast allotted to them.

Impart all needful consolation and support to the poor, the sick, the sorrowful, and the dying. Instruct the ignorant; arouse the careless; strengthen the weak; confirm the wavering. Diffuse the glorious light of Thy Gospel among those who are sitting in darkness and in the shadow of death; and hasten the time when all the kingdoms of the world shall become the kingdoms of the Lord and of His Christ.

Graciously hear our humble supplications, and do to us abundantly above all that we ask or think, through Jesus Christ our Lord.—Amen.

Morning of a Communion Sabbath.

ALMIGHTY GOD, Father of our Lord Jesus Christ, who hast given us through Him free access to Thy presence, and art graciously inviting us, on this Thy holy day, to the worship of Thy house and the fellowship of Thy table; bestow upon us the grace of Thy Holy Spirit, that we may serve Thee acceptably with reverence and godly fear.

Impress our minds, we beseech Thee, with a just sense of all the adorable attributes of Thy character. Fill our hearts with lively gratitude for the countless and unceasing bounties of Thy providence. Above all, let our souls be stirred up to bless Thee for the riches of Thy grace, and to give unto Thee the glory that is due for Thine inestimable love in our redemption.

We magnify and praise Thy holy name for having so loved the world as to give Thine only-begotten Son, that whosoever believeth in Him should not perish, but have everlasting life. We thank Thee that He was made flesh and dwelt among us; that He fulfilled all righteousness, and went about doing good; that He humbled Himself and became obedient unto death, being wounded for our transgressions and bruised for our iniquities; that He rose from the dead, ascended into heaven, and being by the right hand of God exalted, received for us of the Father the promise of the Holy Spirit; that, touched with the feeling of our infirmities, He ever liveth to make intercession for us, and is able to save them to the uttermost who come unto Thee through Him; and that, having gone to prepare a place for His people, He will come again to receive them unto Himself, that where He is there they may be also.

What shall we render unto Thee, O Lord, for all these Thy benefits toward us? We will take the cup of salvation, and call upon Thy holy name, and pay our vows to Thee in the presence of Thy people. O Lord, we will praise Thee; though Thou wast angry with us, Thine anger is turned away, and Thou hast comforted us. Thou hast delivered our souls from death, our eyes from tears, and our feet from falling. Help us to walk before Thee in the land of the living, seeking our rest in Thee, who dealest bountifully with us, and presenting our bodies a living sacrifice, holy and acceptable unto God, which is our reasonable service.

Blessed be Thy name, O God of our salvation, for that renewed opportunity Thou art giving us of observing the holy sacrament of the Supper. Prepare us, we beseech Thee, for this ordinance, according to the preparation of the sanctuary. Confirm our faith in those great mysteries of redeeming grace which we are this day to show forth. Inspire us with ardent love to the Saviour. Work in us unfeigned sorrow for our sins. Give us sincere and humble purposes of new obedience, that we may with a true heart devote ourselves to His service. And enable us, while partaking of this ordinance, to feed by faith on the blessings represented by it, so as to promote our spiritual nourishment and growth in grace.

Bestow Thy favour on all our fellow-worshippers, and grant that they may be united to us in the bonds of charity, as becometh those who are brethren in the Lord. Be very gracious to Thy ministering servants, and give them richly to enjoy in their own souls the comforts and blessings they are honoured to dispense to others. Supply the lack of ordinances to those who are withheld by infirmity or affliction from worshipping in Thy house, and communicating at Thy table. Visit them also with the comforts of Thy fellowship, and satisfy their souls with Thy goodness. Bless Thy Church Universal throughout the world. Let grace, mercy, and peace be multiplied unto all that love the Lord Jesus in sincerity.

And now, O God, our hope is in Thee. If Thy presence go not with us, carry us not up hence. Be with us in all the duties that await us. Make Thy grace sufficient for us. And grant that the words of our mouth, and the meditation of our heart, may be acceptable in Thy sight, through Jesus Christ, our Lord and only Saviour.—Amen.

Evening of a Communion Sabbath.

ALMIGHTY GOD, Father of mercies, from whom cometh down every good and perfect gift, we bless and praise Thy name for all Thy benefits. We thank Thee that Thou hast not only provided for us all things needful to sustain us in the present life, but that Thou art pleased also to feed us with that spiritual food whereby our souls may be nourished unto life eternal.

Fill our hearts with gratitude, we beseech Thee, for what we have this day seen, and heard, and tasted, and handled of the Word of Life; for Jesus Christ, who hath been evidently set forth crucified among us; and for the memorials and pledges of His dying love, of which we have been privileged to partake. Let every good impression made upon us by the solemnities of a communion season be deepened and confirmed. Let the vows and resolutions we have formed at the table of the Lord be remembered and fulfilled. And grant that the spiritual nourishment and comfort we have there received may strengthen us for the duties and trials which await us, so that we may be enabled to go onwards on our way with enlarged and rejoicing hearts.

Help us, O God, in all things to walk worthy of the good confession we have witnessed before many brethren. Suffer us not to return to those sins which we have solemnly renounced as the hateful and accursed things that crucified the Lord of glory. Let us not be neglectful of those duties which we have promised to render to Him, as His ransomed and peculiar people. Enable us always to bear about with us in the body the dying of the Lord Jesus, that the life also of Jesus may be made manifest in our mortal flesh. And grant that the love of Christ may constrain us to live no longer unto ourselves, but unto Him who died for us and rose again.

Gracious Lord, without whom we can do nothing, but through whom we can do all things, restrain us from self-confidence and presumption, and teach us humbly and faithfully to trust in Thee. Hold Thou up our goings in Thy paths, that our footsteps slip not. Enable us to be steadfast and immovable, always abounding in the work of the Lord; that when our course in this life is ended, we may be admitted to the supper of the Lamb, and may sit down with Him in the kingdom of His Father.

We commend to Thy favour our friends and fellow-worshippers, and more especially those who, on this occasion, have joined with us in commemorating the Saviour's death. May their hearts be comforted, being knit together in love. And as they have received Christ Jesus the Lord, so may they walk in Him, rooted and built up in Him, stablished in the faith, and abounding therein with thanksgiving. Be gracious to the young; confirm them in their principles, and keep them from the evil that is in the world. Support the aged under the burden of their infirmities, and cheer them with the persuasion that Thou wilt never leave them nor forsake them.

Abundantly bless Thy ministering servants who have dispensed to us the word and bread of life. Make them the instruments of much good to the souls of others; and grant that in all things their own souls may prosper.

Bestow Thy blessing on Thy whole Church throughout the world. Enlarge, and purify, and stablish it more and more. And hasten the time when the fulness of the Gentiles and the dispersed of Israel shall be gathered into Thy fold.

To Thy fatherly care, O God, we commit ourselves, and all who are near and dear to us, this night; beseeching Thee to defend us from all evil, and to bring us in safety to the light of another day.

And now, O God of peace, who broughtest again from the dead our Lord Jesus, that great Shepherd of the sheep, through the blood of the everlasting covenant; make us perfect in every good work to do Thy will, working in us that which is well-pleasing in Thy sight through Jesus Christ; to whom be glory for ever and ever.—Amen.

First Morning of the Year.

ETERNAL and unchangeable Jehovah, with whom there is no beginning of days or end of years, we humble ourselves, as becometh perishing creatures, in the presence of Him who liveth for ever and ever.

What is man, O God, that Thou art mindful of him, or the son of man that Thou visitest him? Behold, Thou hast made our days as an handbreadth; and our age is as nothing before Thee. As for man, his days are as grass; as the flower of the field, so he flourisheth; for the wind passeth over it and it is gone, and the place thereof shall know it no more. But Thou, the Ancient of Days, art ever the same, and Thy years shall not fail.

Heavenly Father, we look back with gratitude on all the way whereby Thou hast led us, and on all the benefits, temporal and spiritual, which we have continually received at Thy most bountiful hand. From day to day, and from year to year, hast Thou preserved our lives, and supplied our wants, and given us richly all things to enjoy. From manifold evils and dangers Thou hast delivered us; with countless and unceasing benefits Thou hast crowned us; with multiplied advantages and means of grace, though sadly abused and undervalued, Thou hast favoured us; in the midst of much ingratitude and unfaithfulness, and of numberless sins and provocations, Thou hast spared us; and we are all here alive this day, to acknowledge with thankful hearts, that hitherto Thou hast helped us, and that goodness and mercy have followed us all the days of our lives.

Holy Father, we confess before Thee that we are not worthy of the least of all Thy mercies. In many things have we offended; in all things have we come short of Thy glory. The laws which Thou hast prescribed to us we have broken; the benefits Thou hast conferred on us we have forgotten; the warnings and judgments Thou hast sent to us we have neglected; the time and talents Thou hast allotted to us we have wasted; the privileges and advantages Thou hast given us we have misimproved. It is of Thy mercies, O Lord, that we are not consumed, because Thy compassions fail not.

Lord God, merciful and gracious, who hast given Thine only-begotten Son to be the propitiation for our sins, bestow upon us, for His sake, Thy forgiveness, and make the light of Thy countenance to shine upon us. Remember not against us former transgressions; remember Thy tender mercies and loving-kindnesses, for they have been ever of old. And according to Thy mercy remember Thou us, for Thy goodness' sake, O Lord.

Give unto us also the grace of Thy Holy Spirit, whereby we may be enabled to bring forth fruits meet for repentance, and by a sober, righteous, and godly life, to glorify Thy blessed name. Renew us in the spirit of our minds; and grant that with godly sorrow for the past, and with earnest purposes of new obedience for the future, we may think upon our ways, and turn our feet unto Thy testimonies, and make haste to keep Thy commandments.

Impress us, O God, with an abiding sense of the shortness and uncertainty of our lives, and so teach us to number our days that we may apply our hearts unto wisdom. Give us grace to redeem the time we have spent in sloth, vanity, and wickedness, by greater earnestness and diligence in the work of preparation for eternity. Grant that, as our days are multiplied, our holy resolutions may be strengthened; and that, as we draw ever nearer to the grave, we may constantly grow in our conformity to Thine image, and in our meetness to inherit Thy heavenly kingdom.

Into Thy hands, O God, we commit ourselves, beseeching Thee, who hast blessed us hitherto, to bless us still. Prosper us in our lawful undertakings. Keep us from all the evil that is in the world. Prepare us for every event that may befall us. Grant that, whether in prosperity or in adversity, in health or in sickness, in life or in death, we may be upheld and comforted with the assurance that all things work together for good to them that love Thee. And make us to be so rooted and grounded in the faith, and so abundantly fruitful in good works, that in what hour soever our Lord shall come, we may be found of Him in peace, and may receive that crown of righteousness, which is laid up for them that love His appearing.

Graciously hear us, O God, while we plead with Thee, not for ourselves only, but for our fellow-men.

We pray for the diffusion of the Gospel among all nations; for the conversion of the Jews; the enlightenment of the heathens; the downfall of all error, idolatry, and superstition; and the speedy and universal prevalence of the Saviour's kingdom.

We implore Thy blessing on all the Reformed Churches, especially on those which are established in our own land; that truth and godliness may flourish in them more and more; and that their members, united by the bond of charity, may dwell together as brethren in peace.

Bestow Thy favour on the British Empire and all its colonies. Preserve to us our liberties and privileges. Bless our Sovereign and all in authority over us; enable them to rule in Thy fear; and grant that under them all orders of the people may lead quiet lives in godliness and honesty.

We commend our friends to Thy friendship; our benefactors to Thy bounty; our enemies to Thy forgiveness.

We pray for all whom Thou hast visited with affliction, that it may please Thee to comfort and relieve them, and to sanctify their experience of Thy chastening to their eternal profit and joy.

These, our humble supplications, we present to Thee, in the name of Jesus, Thy beloved Son, our Lord and Saviour.—Amen.

Last Evening of the Year.

O GOD, who by Thy merciful providence hast brought us to the close of another year, we lift up our souls to Thee in humble and hearty acknowledgment of Thy benefits. Thou hast heaped them upon us even from our birth, as though we had always done Thy will; and yet we have been so occupied with vain things, that we have never loved, or served, or thanked Thee so heartily for them as we ought to have done. Thy power hath created us; Thy bounty hath sustained us; Thy fatherly discipline hath chastened and corrected us; Thy patience hath borne with us; Thy love hath redeemed us. Verily we are not worthy of the least of all Thy mercies. Justly mightest Thou forsake us, who have often forsaken Thee; and condemn us, whose conscience condemns ourselves. But who can measure Thy goodness, who givest all, and art ready to forgive all!

O Lord, open Thou our lips, and our mouth shall show forth Thy praise. Give us a heart to love and serve Thee. And enable us to show our thankfulness for all the goodness and mercy Thou hast conferred, by giving up ourselves to Thy service, and cheerfully submitting in all things to Thy blessed will.

O God, who hast not appointed us to wrath, but to obtain salvation by our Lord Jesus Christ, blot out for His sake our manifold transgressions, which in thought, word, or deed, we have heretofore committed against Thee. Impute not unto us the sins of our youth; neither reckon with us for the iniquities of our riper years. And, notwithstanding our unworthiness of Thy favour, and our past ingratitude for Thy goodness, con·

tinue to us those temporal and spiritual blessings, which we have hitherto received at Thy most bountiful hand.

O satisfy us early with Thy mercy, that we may rejoice and be glad in Thee all our days. Supply all our need according to Thy glorious riches. And make all grace to be multiplied toward us, that we always, having sufficiency in all things, may abound unto every good work. Teach us also to be careful for nothing, but in everything, by prayer and supplication with thanksgiving, to make our requests known unto Thee; that the peace of God, which passeth all understanding, may keep our hearts and minds through Christ Jesus.

Almighty God, who art daily reminding us, by the warnings of Thy providence, no less than by the lessons of Thy Word, that here we have no continuing city, make us deeply sensible, we beseech Thee, of the shortness and uncertainty of our time on earth. Withdraw our affections from a world which we must soon leave, and in which there is nothing permanent or satisfying. And let Thy Holy Spirit so lead us to walk before Thee in holiness and righteousness all the days of our lives, that, when we have served Thee in our generation, we may depart in peace, and may, through the merits and grace of Thy beloved Son, obtain an eternal inheritance in Thy kingdom.

O God, be merciful unto us, and bless us, and cause Thy face to shine upon us: that Thy way may be known upon earth; Thy saving health among all nations. Let the people praise Thee, O God; let all the people praise Thee. O let the nations be glad, and sing for joy; for Thou shalt judge the people righteously, and govern the nations upon earth. Let the people praise Thee, O God; let all the people praise Thee. Then shall the earth yield her increase; and God, even our own God, shall bless us. God shall bless us; and all the ends of the earth shall fear Him.

Father of mercies, we commend to Thee all those whom Thou art pleased to chasten with any trial or affliction; all nations visited with pestilence, famine, or war; all persons afflicted with poverty, sickness, bondage, or other distress, whether of body or of mind; that it may please Thee to show them Thy fatherly kindness, and to chasten them only for their profit; to the end that, turning with their whole hearts unto Thee, they may receive perfect consolation, and in Thy good time a full deliverance from all their troubles.

And now, O God, we humbly commit ourselves, and those who are near and dear to us, to Thy care; beseeching Thee to watch over us this night, and all the time of our sojourning on earth. God of our fathers, be our God for evermore. Guide us by Thy counsel while we live, and afterward receive us into glory, through Jesus Christ our Lord.—Amen.

Morning Prayer for a Family visited with Sickness or any other Affliction.

O GOD, who art our refuge and our strength, a very present help in trouble, enable us to put our trust in Thee. What time our heart is overwhelmed or in perplexity, lead us to the Rock that is higher than we. And graciously remember Thy Word unto Thy servants, on which Thou hast caused us to hope, that Thou wilt keep him in perfect peace whose mind is stayed upon Thee.

Almighty God, who art pleased in this world to subject us to manifold troubles and distresses, for the exercise of our faith and patience, grant that in the midst of them we may ever remain tranquil, through firm reliance on the promises Thou hast made to us. Though storms should gather around us on every side, suffer us neither to faint through despondency, nor to fall away through unbelief. Enable us steadfastly to look up to Thee, as carrying on the government of the world, not only for the punishment of the ungodly, but for the protection and preservation of Thine own people. Confirm our faith in the assurance Thou hast given us, that all things work together for good to them that love Thee. And enable us to bear patiently such trials as shall befall us, without being disturbed or disquieted in our minds, until we are at length brought to the promised land of rest, where, freed from all troubles, we shall enjoy that eternal blessedness, which Thou hast prepared for us through Jesus Christ our Saviour.

[Gracious God, who hast taught us in Thy Word that Thou dost not willingly afflict the children of men, look with compassion on that member of this family, on whom Thou hast laid Thy chastening hand.

Sanctify to *him* Thy fatherly correction, that it may yield in *him* the peaceable fruits of righteousness. Work in *him* true repentance towards Thee, and faith unfeigned towards the Lord Jesus Christ, so that *he* may obtain forgiveness of *his* sins, and an inheritance among them that are sanctified. Teach *him* to submit with meekness to Thy will; comfort *him* with a persuasion of Thy favour; support *him* with the hope of eternal life.

We earnestly pray that, if it seem good to Thee, Thou wouldst bless the means employed for *his* recovery, that *his* sufferings may be relieved, *his* health restored, and *his* days prolonged to serve Thee on the earth. But if Thou hast appointed that this sickness shall be unto death, prepare *him*, O God, to depart in peace; and mercifully receive *him* into those blessed mansions which Thou art reserving in heaven for the faithful.]

We thank Thee, O God, that Thou hast not appointed us to wrath, but to obtain salvation by our Lord Jesus Christ, who died for us, that, whether we wake or sleep, we should live together with Him. Help us, we pray Thee, with true faith to rest upon Him, and all our life long with purpose of heart to cleave to Him; that being redeemed with His most precious blood, and sanctified by the grace of His Holy Spirit, we may, in all our trials, be supported by a comfortable persuasion of Thy love, and a lively hope of inheriting Thy glorious kingdom.

Father of mercies, extend Thy compassion to all Thy people whom Thou hast visited with affliction. Supply their wants. Relieve their sufferings. Enable them to bow in meek submission to Thy will. And let Thy fatherly chastening be conducive to their growth in grace and preparation for eternity.

And now, O God, we humbly commit ourselves, and those whom we love, to Thy care. Defend us alike from all adversities which may befall the body, and from all temptations which may assault and hurt the soul. Prepare us for every event which may befall us. And grant that, whether in health or in sickness, in joy or in grief, in life or in death, we may be enabled to glorify Thy name, through Jesus Christ our Lord.—Amen.

Evening Prayer for a Family visited with Sickness or any other Affliction.

O LORD our God, who inhabitest eternity, but dwellest also with the humble and contrite spirit, incline Thine ear to the voice of our supplications. Although we are unworthy to come into Thy presence, or to receive any blessing at Thy hands, yet let it please Thee favourably to regard us, through the merits and mediation of Thy beloved Son. Hide Thy face, we beseech Thee, from our sins, and blot out all our iniquities. Put not away Thy servants in anger; Thou hast been our help; leave us not, neither forsake us, O God of our salvation. Work in us, by the grace of Thy Holy Spirit, that broken and penitent heart which Thou dost not despise. And mercifully fulfil to us Thy promise, that Thou wilt not contend for ever, neither wilt Thou be always wroth, lest the spirit should fail before Thee, and the souls which Thou hast made.

Almighty God, who orderest all things in heaven and earth according to Thy wise counsel, give us grace that we may reverently adore, and cheerfully submit to Thy most blessed will. Teach us to acknowledge that Thou art just in all Thy ways, and holy in all Thy works. And however mysterious Thy dealings with us may seem to be, cause us to be persuaded in our hearts that Thy judgments are right, and that in faithfulness Thou hast afflicted us. Convince us that we are not worthy of the least of all Thy mercies, and that we have no cause to murmur when Thy gracious gifts are withheld or withdrawn from us. Confirm our faith in Thee as our reconciled God, whose just anger hath in Christ Jesus been turned away, and whose thoughts towards us are thoughts of peace, and not of evil. Teach us to know Him whom we have believed, so as to be persuaded that He is able to keep unto the great day that which we have committed to Him. And satisfy our souls with the assurance, that neither death nor life, nor angels, nor principalities, nor powers, nor things present, nor things to come, nor height, nor depth, nor any other creature, shall be able to separate us from the love of God, which is in Christ Jesus our Lord.

[O God, in whose hand is the life of all mankind, and the breath of every living thing, look with compassion on that member of this family, for whom, in *his* time of sore trouble, we intercede.

Lord, rebuke *him* not in Thine anger, neither chasten *him* in Thy hot displeasure. Turn Thou unto *him* and have mercy on *him*, for *he* is desolate and afflicted. The troubles of *his* heart are enlarged; O bring Thou *him* out of *his* distresses.

We know, O Lord, that nothing is too hard for Thee, and that, if Thou wilt, Thou art able to make *him* whole. Arrest, we beseech Thee, the progress of *his* disease. Bless the means employed for its removal. And spare *him*, that *he* may recover strength before *he* go hence and be no more. But whatever may be Thy purpose with respect to *him*, enable *him* to say, The will of the Lord be done. And graciously prepare *him* for what may be awaiting *him*, that whether *he* live or die, *he* may be Thine.

Grant to Thy servant a truly penitent heart for all the sins *he* hath at any time committed, together with a lively faith in Thy Son Jesus Christ, who is able to save *him* unto the uttermost; so that the transgressions of *his* past life may be blotted out, and the joys and comforts of Thy favour may be restored to *him*. Let Thy Holy Spirit be shed on *him* abundantly, to strengthen *him* for the endurance of *his* sufferings, to purify *him* from all remaining sin, and to witness that *he* is a child of God and an heir of heaven. And if it be Thy will at this time to remove *him* from us, grant *him* a peaceful departure out of this life, and graciously receive *him* into those heavenly mansions, where the souls of them that sleep in the Lord Jesus enjoy perpetual rest, and blessedness in Thy presence.]

O God, who art very pitiful and of tender mercy, look with compassion on all Thine afflicted people. Assuage their grief; relieve their sufferings; and overrule Thy chastening for their good.

Extend Thy favour to all our brethren of mankind. Our heart's desire and prayer is that they may be saved.

And now, O God, we humbly commit ourselves, and all whom we love, to Thy fatherly care. Fulfil to us Thy promise, that Thou wilt never leave us nor forsake us. And let the peace of God, which passeth all understanding, keep our hearts and minds, through Jesus Christ; to whom, with Thee, and with the Holy Spirit, be glory everlasting.—Amen.

Morning Prayer for a Bereaved Family.

FATHER of mercies and God of all consolation, we thank Thee that we are encouraged in times of sorrow to lift up our souls unto Thee. Lord, to whom shall we go? Thou hast the words of eternal life.

Look with compassion, we beseech Thee, on this family, from whom Thou hast taken away one that was dear to them. Enable us to say, The will of the Lord be done. Cause us to be persuaded in our hearts, that though this dispensation be mysterious, it is sent in love, and fraught with mercy. And let Thy fatherly chastening be sanctified, to the weaning of our affections from a vain world, and to our greater meetness for that better country, where sorrow and disappointment are unknown.

O blessed Saviour, who didst Thyself weep beside the grave of a beloved friend, fulfil to us Thy promise, that Thou wilt not leave us comfortless. Turn not away Thine ear from our cry; hold not Thy peace at our tears. Say to us with power, Let not your heart be troubled; ye believe in God, believe also in Me. Make Thyself known to us as the Resurrection and the Life; and satisfy our souls with the assurance, that whosoever believeth in Thee, though he were dead, yet shall he live for ever.

Blessed be Thou, O God and Father of our Lord Jesus Christ, who, according to Thine abundant mercy, hast begotten us again unto a lively hope by the resurrection of Jesus Christ from the dead; to an inheritance incorruptible, and undefiled, and that fadeth not away, reserved for us in heaven. Keep us, O Lord, by Thy divine power through faith unto the salvation, which is ready to be revealed in the last time. Enable us therein greatly to rejoice, though now for a season, if need be, we are in heaviness through manifold temptations. And grant that the trial of our faith, being much more precious than of gold that perisheth, though it be tried with fire, may be found unto praise and honour and glory at the appearing of Jesus Christ.

O God, who, by the removal of a departed friend, art showing us that in the midst of life we are in death; grant that we may be rightly impressed by this affecting visitation of Thy providence; and that, by Thy grace, it may make us more earnest in redeeming the time and preparing for eternity. Spare us, merciful Father, yet a little while, before we go hence and be no more. Make us glad according to the days wherein Thou hast afflicted us, and the years wherein we have seen evil. Cause Thy goodness and mercy to follow us all the days of our life; and receive us at last to dwell in Thy house for ever.

O God of peace, who hast loved Thy people, and hast given them everlasting consolation and good hope through grace, we humbly commend to Thee all our brethren in affliction. Comfort and relieve them according to their necessities. And strengthen them with might, according to Thy glorious power, unto all patience and long-suffering with joyfulness.

Look with compassion, we beseech Thee, on all mankind. Promote their peace, their liberty, their happiness. Above all, bring them to the knowledge of the truth, and bless them with the hopes and comforts of Thy Gospel.

Graciously hear us, O God, and have mercy on us, through Jesus Christ our Lord.—Amen.

Evening Prayer for a Bereaved Family.

O LORD, whom have we in heaven but Thee? and there is none upon earth that we desire besides Thee. Our heart and our flesh faileth, but Thou art the strength of our heart, and our portion for ever.

Under the shadow of Thy judgments we come to Thee, seeking Thy grace to support us in our time of trial. O God, who art able to supply every loss, to heal every wound, and to dry up every tear, grant that as our sorrows have abounded, our consolations may much more abound. May we be still and know that thou art God, acknowledging Thy right to do with us as Thou willest, and confiding in the wisdom and goodness of Thy dispensations. Reveal Thyself to us, even when Thou smitest us, as a reconciled God and Father in Christ Jesus, who chastenest us, not for Thy pleasure, but for our profit, and makest all things work together for our good. Cause us to trust in the sympathy of Thy beloved Son, who is ever touched with the feeling of our infirmities; and to rejoice in Him as the Captain of our salvation, who hath redeemed us from the curse of the law, and overcome the sharpness of death, and opened the kingdom of heaven to all believers. Give to us Thy Holy Spirit as our Comforter, to stablish our hearts in the faith of Thy promises, and to strengthen us with might, according to Thy glorious power, unto all patience and long-suffering with joyfulness. And enable us to look beyond this vale of tears to that land of everlasting blessedness and rest, where those Christian friends whom death has for a while severed, shall be for ever united in the presence of their Lord.

We pray that this chastening, though for the present grievous, may in due time yield in us the peaceable fruits of righteousness. May it show us the vanity of all earthly good, and the need we have of a better and more enduring substance. May it lead us to seek a closer union with Thee, from whose love nothing in life or in death can ever divide us. May it teach us to reflect more seriously than we have ever done on the short and uncertain duration of our pilgrimage, and with greater earnestness and diligence than hitherto to lay up in store a good foundation for eternity.

O that we all were wise, that we understood this, that we would consider our latter end. Keep us ever mindful that this world is not our rest. Teach us, as strangers and pilgrims on the earth, to desire a better country, that is, a heavenly, and to pass the time of our sojourning in Thy fear, so that, when it shall be Thy will to call us hence, we may have a peaceful departure out of this life, in favour with Thee, and in perfect charity with all mankind, and may be received into that heavenly kingdom, which Thou hast prepared for them that love Thee.

And now, O Lord, what wait we for? our hope is in Thee. Enable us to cast upon Thee all our care, whether for ourselves or for any who are dear to us, in the full persuasion that Thou carest for us. And let the peace of God, which passeth all understanding, keep our hearts and minds, through Jesus Christ; to whom, with Thee, and with the Holy Ghost, be glory everlasting.—Amen.

www.ingramcontent.com/pod-product-compliance
Lightning Source LLC
Chambersburg PA
CBHW032131160426

43197CB00008B/602